Race, Gender, and Leadership

Re-Envisioning Organizational Leadership
From the Perspectives of African
American Women Executives

Race, Gender, and Leadership

Re-Envisioning Organizational Leadership From the Perspectives of African American Women Executives

Patricia S. Parker, PhD
The University of North Carolina at Chapel Hill

LAWRENCE ERLBAUM ASSOCIATES, PUBLISHERS
2005   Mahwah, New Jersey   London

Lawrence Erlbaum Associates, Inc., Publishers
10 Industrial Avenue
Mahwah, New Jersey 07430

Cover design by Sean Trane Sciarrone

Library of Congress Cataloging-in-Publication Data

Parker, Patricia Sue, 1958–
    Race, gender, and leadership : re-envisioning organizational leadership from the perspectives of African American women executives / Patricia S. Parker.
       p. cm.
    Includes bibliographical references and index.
    ISBN 0-8058-4919-x (c. : alk. Paper)
       1. African American women executives. 2. African American women in the professions. 3. Leadership in women—United States.   I. Title.

HD6054.4.U6P37 2004 2005
303.3'4'082—dc22
                                                         2004043265
                                                              CIP

Books published by Lawrence Erlbaum Associates are printed on acid-free paper, and their bindings are chosen for strength and durability.

Printed in the United States of America
10   9   8   7   6   5   4   3   2   1

To my son
Patrick Benjamin Anderson

In memory of my parents
Alice Walker Parker and Pardie Parker

and

In honor of the
African American women whose lives
provide the inspiration for this book

Contents

Preface

Much has been written about a model of leadership that emphasizes women's values and experiences that is in some ways distinct from male models of leadership. This book redirects the focus to a view of leadership as a multicultural phenomenon that moves beyond dualistic notions of "masculine" and "feminine" leadership, and focuses more specifically on leadership as the management of meaning, including the meanings of the notion of *organizational leader*. Specifically, this book takes up the charge put forth by cutting edge leadership scholars to envision new forms of leadership for the 21st century (see Avolio & Bass, 2002; Greenleaf, 1977; Rost, 1991; Wheatley, 1992).

The focus is on leadership traditions revealed in the history of Black women in America and exemplified in the leadership approaches of 15 African American women executives who came of age during the civil rights and feminist movements of the 1960s and 1970s, and climbed to the top of major U.S. organizations. This volume advances a vision of organizational leadership that challenges traditional masculine and feminine notions of leadership development and practice, providing insights for organizational leadership in the era of postindustrialization and globalization. Additionally, by placing African American women at the center of analysis, this book provides insights into the ways in which race and gender structure key leadership processes in today's diverse and changing workplace.

ACKNOWLEDGMENTS

The work for this book could not have been completed without the support of many people. First I want to thank my colleagues at The University of North

Carolina at Chapel Hill, Department of Communication Studies, for their encouragement and support throughout the various stages of this project. I am especially grateful to my Department Chair, V. William Balthrop, for his continued guidance. Thanks also to Linda Bathgate and her colleagues at Lawrence Erlbaum Associates, whose professionalism and keen insight were instrumental in moving this project from the proposal stage through publication. Likewise, this work benefited immensely from the cogent and thorough analysis by the reviewers, and the expert guidance of the Communication Series Editor, Jennings Bryant, and Advisory Editor, Linda L. Putnam.

Of course, this book could not have been completed without the African American women executives and their coworkers who participated in this study. I am grateful to them for their time, graciousness, and inspiration.

Finally, I am blessed with the support of a loving family and extended community that have encouraged me throughout the process of writing this book. To my family at St. Paul AME Church, especially my prayer partners Marion Brooks, Glenda Harris, and Johnnie Ponder, thank you for helping me keep the faith. To my sisters, May, Jurlene, Zora, Helen, Carolyn, Willette, Debra, and Mary, thank you for the love that continues to bind us and for affirming for me everyday the power of Black women. To my brothers, Eric, Richard, Alvin, and George, thank you for your love and encouragement and for being a constant source of strength for me. Finally, and most importantly, to my son, Patrick, I thank you for your unconditional love, and for sharing your magnificence with me.

Introduction[1]

RE-ENVISIONING LEADERSHIP
IN THE POSTINDUSTRIAL ERA

Whom should we study to learn about leadership in organizations of the 21st century? In the past, the defining group for conceptualizing leadership develop-ment and practice, as well as other organizational theories and constructs, has been White[2] middle-class men (Nkomo, 1992). More recently, as organiza-tional researchers began to study women in management, concurrently creat-ing the massive gender and leadership literature, the focus was still limited to predominantly one group, White middle-class women (Bell & Nkomo, 1992, 2001; Nkomo, 1988). Thus in the leadership literature there exists two compet-ing models of leadership, based almost exclusively on studies of White women and men, that are presented as race neutral and assumed generalized to all peo-ple (Parker & ogilvie, 1996). One model is based on the notion of masculine in-strumentality, and the other is based on the notion of feminine collaboration. Both models are grounded within perspectives that assume racial neutrality, while privileging White middle-class cultural norms and values reinforced through gender symbolism that operates as the universal depiction of men and women across cultural and class boundaries.

In the new millennium, as Johnston and Packer's (1987) forecast of an increasingly diverse workforce becomes a reality, organizations would benefit from re-envisioning leadership from the multicultural perspectives of the workforce and moving past the *either/or*, race-neutral thinking manifested in current gender and leadership research. Studying diverse perspectives of leadership forces us to take seriously the claim that with organizational diversity comes fresh perspectives on traditional organizational communication issues (Allen, 1995) and a richer pool of resources for creating desired outcomes. This book calls attention to one under-represented leadership perspective, that of African American[3] women executives.

Placing African American women at the center of analysis provides a vantage point from which to examine how race and gender intersect with organizational leadership theory development. The race-neutral theorizing underlying previous models has influenced who gets included in studies about leadership (e.g., women of color are systematically excluded) and the kinds of questions that are asked about leadership behaviors (e.g., cultural assumptions about feminine and masculine leadership are rarely called into question). Moreover, incorporating the tradition of resistance and transformation exemplified in African American women's traditions of leadership signals a shift from industrial visions of leadership that have focused on race-neutral, dichotomized notions of masculine and feminine leadership.

The Call for New Visions of Leadership in the Postindustrial Era

The central premise of this book is that focusing on African American women's organizational leadership provides a way of re-envisioning leadership in the era of postindustrialization and globalization. Several scholars have argued persuasively that 21st leadership requires new perspectives that signal a shift from the values and cultural norms of the industrial paradigm—that is, rational, management oriented, self-interested, cost-benefit driven, hierarchical, and expressive individualism (Deetz, 2003; Deetz, Tracy, & Simpson, 2000; Greenleaf, 1977; Rost, 1991). In his comprehensive critique, Rost (1991) argued that mainstream leadership theories grounded in the leadership mythology of the industrial paradigm—for example, having one person take charge and directing from a distance (in the tradition of a John Wayne character or General George Patton)—may have served their purposes since the 1930s, but they "increasingly ill [serve] the needs of a world rapidly being transformed by a massive paradigm shift in societal values" (p.181).

Leadership approaches for the 21st century must be grounded in values and norms that are more relevant in the postindustrial era of rapid change and globalization. Deetz, Tracy, and Simpson (2000) argued that important social changes and changes in the nature of products and work processes have created a crises of control in contemporary organizations. They cite such changes as the rise of professionalized workplaces, geographically dispersed facilities, decentralization, and turbulent markets that have contributed to the difficulty of coordination and control. These changes signal a shift toward more ambiguous communication contexts, in which identities and relationships are not fixed but must be negotiated (Fairclough, 1992).

Increasingly, there is need to shift away from the myth of the triumphant individual, "the larger-than-life individual working alone," and begin focusing on new approaches, such as creative collaboration, teamwork, and coalition building and maintenance within and among organizations (Bennis & Biederman, 1997, p. 2). These new approaches to organizing point to the need for norms and values such as concern for a common good, diversity and pluralism in structures and participation, client orientation, and consensus-oriented policy-making process more relevant in the postindustrial era (Rost, 1991). Leadership in the context of 21st-century organizing must be viewed as a process that facilitates the development of these more relevant norms.

This volume offers a view of leadership derived from a study of African American women executives that expresses these more relevant themes. Moreover, this view is presented an exemplar of a meaning-centered approach to leadership, which I argue is needed to address the complex and ambiguous context of 21st-century organizations and that can help us to see past the either/or, race-neutral thinking perpetuated in gender and leadership studies. Scholars in communication and organizational development on the cutting edge of thinking about postindustrial leadership models emphasize meaning-centered approaches (Avolio & Bass, 2002; Deetz et al., 2000; Fairhurst & Sarr, 1996; Parker, 2001; Rost 1991; Smircich & Morgan, 1982; Witherspoon, 1997). Meaning-centered approaches reflect a critical interpretive view of reality and provide the potential for a multifaceted feminist framework that advances new approaches to leadership and new sources of leadership knowledge. A critical interpretive view of leadership shifts the focus away from structural-functionalist, management-oriented views and toward the process of leadership that develops through meaningful interaction, and how it can facilitate social change and emancipation (Foster, 1989). In the postindustrial era of rapid change and globalization, process, social change, and emancipation are fundamental elements for defining leadership in the postindustrial area (Deetz et al., 2000; Foster, 1989; Rost, 1991).

Defining Leadership in the Postindustrial Area

In this volume I combine two definitions of leadership that reflect a meaning-centered approach and capture the process, change, and emancipatory elements necessary for the postindustrial era. These definitions are discussed in Chapter 3 of this volume, but I describe them briefly here. First is Smircich and

Morgan's (1982) definition of leadership, which effectively describes leadership as the management of meaning. To Smircich and Morgan's (1982) definition, I add Rost's (1991) concept of leadership that builds on Burns (1978) ground-breaking notion of leadership transformation, but with a critical eye toward postindustrial assumptions and values that Burn's definition does not address. Rost's (1991) definition builds on Smircich and Morgan's conceptualization of leadership as the creation of meaning through interaction; however, his definition places a critical emphasis on social change and emancipation.

Taken together, these definitions conceptualize leadership as a localized, negotiated process of mutual influence that would theoretically accommodate the multiple, often contradictory, viewpoints and paradoxical situational challenges of 21st-century organizations (Parker, 2001). If organizational leadership should be understood as a process of negotiating meaning within contradictory and paradoxical situations to bring about social change, then we would do well to listen closely to what the experiences of African American women leaders reveal.

Uncovering a Tradition of African American Women's Leadership

Contemporary African American women's organizational leadership is grounded in a tradition of survival, resistance, and change that, historically, has been ignored or devalued. African American women's tradition of leadership began as a form of creative resistance and community building during the era of slavery, and more recently was revealed in the experiences of African American women who were the invisible leaders of the civil rights movement (see Hine & Thompson, 1998; Payne, 1995). Women such as Ella Baker and Fannie Lou Hammer, along with other unnamed African American women, were skilled organizers who were instrumental in building and sustaining the early years of the civil rights movement. Today, African American women leaders who came of age during that turbulent era, such as Anne Fudge, chairwoman and chief executive at advertising giant Young & Rubicam, national security advisor Condoleezza Rice, and Brown University president, Ruth Simmons, have leadership positions in some of the top U.S. corporations and public organizations. Additionally, the grassroots community organizing of African American women living in neighborhoods where they must protect their children from gang violence and other crime rooted in the illicit drug economy, is transforming traditional concepts of community development (Gittell, Ortega-Bustamante, & Steffy, 1999; Stack, 2000; Stall & Stoecker, 1998). However, a "tradition" of African American women's leadership is absent in the leadership literature in general.[4] For example the popular series, *Hartwick Classic Leadership Cases* (2003), which introduced its "women as leaders" series in 1994, includes no examples of African American women leaders.

More conspicuously, African American women are virtually excluded in the gender and leadership literature (Parker & ogilvie, 1996). Indeed, one of the most popular feminist perspectives on leadership actually contributes to the silencing of some women as potential leaders, including, but not limited to, African American women. The so-called "female advantage" model of leadership described in feminist studies of women in management and advanced in the popular press, argues that a "distinctly feminine" style of leadership makes women better leaders than men (Helgesen, 1990, Lunneborg, 1990; Rosener, 1990). From this perspective, researchers have focused on the identity and experiences of a select few—almost exclusively White, middle-class women—and created a theory of "feminine leadership" that is meant to generalize to the experiences of all women (cf., Helgesen, 1990, Lunneborg, 1990; Rosener, 1990). The female advantage perspective excludes the experiences of African American women, as well as other women of color and of different class statuses.

The exclusion of African American women from both traditional and feminist studies of leadership is in part a by-product of the problems of race-neutral theorizing in organization studies. In order to envision a more inclusive framework for understanding leadership in the 21st century, we must move beyond race-neutral theorizing in conceptualizing important cultural processes, such as leadership.

Beyond Race-Neutral Theorizing in Organizational Communication

Recently, a number of researchers have called attention to the persistence of race-neutral theorizing in organizational communication (Ashcraft & Allen, 2003; Flores & Moon, 2002; Grimes, 2002; Parker, 2001, 2003; Taylor & Trujillo, 2001). These scholars pointed out that despite the comparatively sustained critique of organizations as fundamentally gendered (Allen, 1995, 1996, 1998; Bullis, 1993; Buzzanell, 1994, 2000; Marshall, 1993; Mumby, 1993; Mumby & Putnam, 1992; Trethewey, 1997), researchers have not taken up the issue of organizations as fundamentally raced (see Ashcraft & Allen, 2003; Parker, 2003). The arguments about the persistence of race-neutral theorizing in organizational communication build on those articulated by Nkomo (1992) in her critique of organization and management studies.

In her groundbreaking essay, *The Emperor Has No Clothes: Rewriting "Race in Organizations,"* Nkomo (1992) demonstrated that scholars persistently conceptualize organizations as race neutral when, in fact, race is and has been present in organizations all along—an illusion she likens to the one created in Hans Christian Andersen's (1837/1968) children's fairy tale, *The Emperor's New Clothes*. In the tale, the emperor's tailors present a magnificent set of clothes, allegedly invisible to those unworthy of having the ability to see them. Although the emperor, his court suitors, and his tailors recognize that he is naked, no one will explicitly acknowledge that nakedness, even as he struts through the streets of the kingdom in a grand procession. When a child in the crowd proclaims the emperor's nakedness, the emperor and his suitors continue with the procession even more proudly than before. In applying this allegory to the silencing of race in organization studies, Nkomo explained:

> [T]he emperor is not simply an emperor but the embodiment of the concept of Western knowledge as both universal and superior and [W]hite males as the defining group for studying organizations. The court suitors are the organizational scholars who continue the traditions of ignoring race and ethnicity in their research and excluding other voices. All have a vested interest in continuing the procession and not calling attention to the omissions.... Even as ... voices [of the other, the excluded, assumed to be childlike and inferior] point to the omissions and errors and the need for inclusiveness, the real issue is getting truly heard, rather than simply added on. (pp. 488–489)

Thus the problems associated with race-neutral theorizing in organization studies are ones related to *domination* (taken-for-granted assumptions about superiority and inferiority), *exclusion* (of certain groups from the knowledge production process), and *containment* (practices that silence those who speak out against or in other ways resist oppression [Collins, 1998a]). The race-neutral view reflects particular historical and social meanings of race that perpetuate systems of domination based on notions of inferiority and superiority (Keto, 1989; Minnich, 1990; Nkomo, 1992; Omi & Winant, 1986). This dominant racial ideology is embedded within a Eurocentric patriarchal view of the world wherein dominant group members (White, heterosexual, middle-class males) are not only constructed as the defining group, but they are

> taken to be the highest category "the best" and all other groups must be defined and judged solely with reference to that hegemonic category.... Other racial and ethnic groups are relegated to subcategories; their experiences are seen as outside of the mainstream of developing knowledge of organizations. (Nkomo, 1992, p. 489)

Alternative views of organizational reality are obscured by the majority of research that privileges White, middle-class male domination. Calàs (1987) made the point that male-dominated hegemonic orientation prevails not by overt domination or resigned acceptance, but by naturalization, by a general recognition that "this is the way things are, and they cannot be any other way" (p. 209).

Race-neutral theorizing in organization science has influenced the study of leadership in significant ways. It has influenced who gets included in studies about leadership, the kinds of questions that are asked about leadership behaviors, and how leadership processes are conceptualized. Like the emperor's court suitors, researchers in organization studies have not traditionally raised issues that would illuminate the reproduction of race-neutral organizations (Cavanaugh, 1997; Nkomo, 1992; Parker, 2001, 2003). Instead, research in organization studies is dominated by an ethnicity paradigm that sustains the dominant racial ideology (Nkomo, 1992). The ethnicity paradigm sets up the dualistic oppositional categories of assimilation versus pluralism to address questions of discrimination and racism. Much of this research is narrowly focused, ahistorical, and decontexualized, and race is treated as a demographic variable (Nkomo, 1992).

Assimilationalism centers on questions of why so-called racial minorities are not becoming incorporated or assimilated into mainstream society. This perspective often leads to a "blame the victim" explanation of why certain groups have not been assimilated (Omi & Winant, 1986). In contrast, pluralists purportedly allow for the possibility that groups do not assimilate but remain distinct in terms of cultural identity. However, "similar to users of assimilation theory, proponents of cultural pluralism still maintain the existence of an allegedly 'normal' (understood to mean superior) majority culture, to which other groups are juxtaposed" (Nkomo, 1992, p. 497). The net effect of research dominated by the ethnicity paradigm is that "there is little awareness that racial minorities may have something to contribute to organizations or that perhaps race can inform our understanding of organizations in other ways" (Nkomo, 1992, p. 500).

Within the ethnicity paradigm, leadership studies have not seriously examined African American women as leaders. For example, research on leadership development that treats White male privilege as a standard would not envision research questions that would incorporate resistance to oppression as a component of leadership development. Also, by focusing on gendered leadership as race-neutral, universal conceptualizations of feminine and masculine leadership do not lead to research questions that would investigate whether feminine and masculine leadership behaviors have multiple cultural meanings that might transcend the feminine–masculine dichotomy. Furthermore, and perhaps most fundamentally, research that sustains the dominant racial ideology would not conceptualize leadership processes in ways that would illuminate tensions, contradictions, and racial conflicts lying just beneath the surface of supposedly race neutrality in organizations.

However, with an eye toward inclusiveness, critical feminist scholars in organizational communication are particularly well situated to illuminate the reproduction of race neutrality in organizations and to envision the study of leadership in ways that take both race and gender into account.

Toward an Inclusive Framework for Envisioning Race, Gender, and Leadership

An inclusive framework for envisioning race, gender, and leadership necessarily employs intersectionality as a guiding principle for analysis. *Intersectionality* is "an analysis claiming that systems of race, economic class, gender, sexuality, ethnicity, nation, and age form mutually constructing features of social organization" (Collins, 1998a, p. 278). In the present analysis, I focus on gender and race as two influential systems that form mutually constructing features of organizational leadership. Empirical and theoretical work in organizational studies has focused almost exclusively on gendered patterns of organizing (cf., Calàs & Smircich, 1996). Acker's (1990) theory of gendered organization is one of the most comprehensive models (cf., Kanter, 1977; Marshall, 1993). Acker's framework draws attention to the everyday social processes in which "advantage and disadvantage, exploitation and control, action and emotion, meaning and identity" (p. 167) are patterned through and in terms of gender. The sole focus on gender, however, masks the fundamental influences of race and other systems of domination in women's work experiences (Amott & Matthaei, 1996; Essed, 1991, 1994; Rowe, 2000; Spelman, 1988). Yoder and Aniakudo (1997) pointed out, following Spelman, that "there is no raceless, classless, generic woman" (p. 325). Thus, the focus should be on the ways multiple systems of domination intersect in everyday interactions.

In this volume, I use critical communication and feminist theories to advance an inclusive framework for envisioning race, gender, and leadership. Critical communication perspectives direct attention to organization as intersubjective structures of meaning where identity and power relationships are produced, maintained, and reproduced through the ongoing communicative practices of its members (Deetz, 1992; Mumby, 2001). Connections among power, ideology, and hegemony are central to this view of organizational communication. *Power* is viewed as a dialectical process of domination (control) and resistance that is manifested in everyday organizational life. *Hegemonic* control functions not simply as ideological domination of one group by another, but as "a dynamic conception of the lived relations of social groups and the various struggles that constantly unfold between and among these groups" (Mumby, 2001, p. 598). This directs attention to the tensions between organization as text (e.g., as discursively produced institutional forms) and organizing as conversation (e.g. how women and men struggle to "do difference").

From a critical communication perspective, gender and race are not neutral elements but can be seen as constitutive of organizing and are primary ways of signifying power in social systems (Acker, 1991; Scott, 1986). Power and control are manifested in the hidden microprocesses and micropractices that produce and reproduce unequal and persistent, sex-, race-, and class-based patterns in work situations such as recruitment, hiring, placement, promotions, and everyday interaction (Parker, 2003). Feminist theories, particularly poststructuralist approaches, enable the deconstruction of raced and gendered organizational leadership contexts, emphasizing the unstable, complex, and ambiguous nature of social reality (Calàs & Smircich, 1996). This directs attention to leadership as a process by which organizational members—leaders and followers—struggle to create meaning within such contexts.

Leadership processes and interaction provide a particularly good case for exploring the tensions and paradoxes of contemporary organization. Executive leadership represents an interaction context in which dominant culture norms and values regarding gender and race take on high symbolic importance (Biggart & Hamilton, 1984). Organizational members come to expect leaders to look, act, and think in ways consistent with the socially constructed meanings of organizational leader and leadership. Traditionally, those meanings have been in conflict with stereotypical assumptions about African American women (Parker, 2001). Thus, exploring the leadership experiences of African American women serves to make salient how race and gender intersect with key organizational leadership issues and processes in 21st-century organizations, and it provides insight into an approach to leadership I theorize is borne out of a struggle to balance the tensions and paradoxes of resisting and conforming to discourses of organizing.

OVERVIEW OF THE STUDY OF AFRICAN AMERICAN WOMEN EXECUTIVES

This book offers a model of leadership derived from a field study involving 15 African American women executives, their subordinates, co-workers, and (in four cases) their immediate supervisors (usually the company CEO or equivalent). It is further informed by a study of a tradition of leadership as revealed in African American women's history. Because I am interested in organizational leadership, my literature search included historical accounts of African American women's experiences in work contexts and also in community organizing. My main sources were well-documented books and articles that used primary sources in addition to secondary sources. The historical grounding of the African American women executives' leadership approach is based on the idea that Black women's experiences in systems of raced, gendered, and classed power relationships in American institutions provide a particular angle of vision from which to forge new understandings about leadership for 21st-century organizations.

Recruitment of Participants

The initial research for this study was completed in 1995, with some follow-up interviews conducted in 2000. To identify participants for the study, I used criteria consistent with those used by other researchers interested in top management leadership (e.g. Mainiero, 1994; Rosener, 1990). Participants for the study met the following criteria: (a) at the level of director or above; (b) had line responsibility; and (c) had supervisory responsibilities. I added a fourth criterion, (d) employed in a major U.S.-dominant culture organization. The fourth criterion coincides with my interest in organizational leadership from the perspective of African American women in systems of raced and gendered power relationships.

A modified snowball technique was used to recruit study participants. A listing of women who fit the sampling criteria was obtained from sources in the popular press (*Black Enterprise Magazine, Ebony, Working Woman*, and *Fortune*) that published lists of women in top management positions. Names of other women were obtained through personal contacts, networking at professional conferences, and through executives who participated in the study. Through these sources a total of 70 African American women executives who fit the criteria were identified. Three of these potential participants chose not to take part in the study when contacted. Further limitations on recruitment included the time-intensive study procedures and budgetary constraints on travel. The final data set was 15 African American women executives in five states and in Washington DC.

Of the 15 executives, 13 were in senior management positions (e.g., vice president or equivalent), and two were in upper middle management (e.g. director or equivalent). Seven executives worked at organizations in the southern region of the United States (Arkansas, Louisiana, Tennessee), five were in the southeast (Georgia and Washington, D. C.), and three were in the Pacific southwest (California). About half the executives worked in private organizations, and half were in the public sector.

Procedure

Data were collected through life history interviews with each executive, semistructured interviews with the executive's subordinates and, when available, her boss, and direct observation of the executive in interaction. Three separate interview protocols were developed for each of these three groups of participants (see the interview protocols in Appendix A). Because I was interested in understanding leadership communication as the management of meaning, the questions for all three protocols contained sections designed to solicit descriptions of interaction involving the executives, their co-workers, subordinates, and clients. The interviews lasted an average of 1 hour, and ranged from 45 minutes to 2½ hours. Some of the women are public figures, so I was able to supplement their life history interviews with published biographical data. I also used archival data, such as samples of internal and external communications, publications, memos, speeches, daily schedules, and corporate media. The use of multiple research procedures is common in field studies designed to generate new theories in understudied areas. This provides opportunities for verifying emerging ideas as the research progresses (Strauss & Corbin, 1990).

The African American women executives who participated in this research provided provocative narratives that detailed their views as "outsiders within" (Collins, 1990) some of the top corporations and public institutions in the United States. Their life histories, combined with descriptions of their leadership communication by their subordinates, supervisors, and other co-workers, give insight into an approach to leadership development and practice that inform new visions of leadership in the 21st century.

OVERVIEW OF THIS BOOK

This book is presented in three parts. Part I establishes the need for race- and gender-inclusive visions of organizational leadership in the postindustrial era and provides a rationale for a theory of leadership rooted in meaning-centered approaches. The section is divided into chapters that together build a rationale for re-envisioning leadership for 21st-century organizations.

Chapter 1 uses a critical communication perspective to review and critique the predominant visions of leadership in both the traditional and feminist literature. The chapter demonstrates how race neutral theorizing in this literature reinforces idealized images of a White female and male ideal in leadership theory and practice, ultimately limiting our ability to envision leadership more complexly. Moreover, traditional models and certain feminist approaches set up particular ways of envisioning leadership communication that are less well-suited to meeting the challenges of 21st-century organizations. The chapter proposes an inclusive critical feminist framework for studying race, gender, and leadership in the 21st century.

Chapter 2 uses the established critical feminist framework to advance a meaning-centered view of leadership communication. This shifts the focus to the leadership process as localized, negotiated and socially constructed, and embraces a both/and orientation that goes beyond rigid reified dualities such as masculine versus feminine leadership styles. It is a vision of leadership that would accommodate the multicultural, racialized, and contradictory viewpoints and paradoxical situational challenges of 21st-century organization.

Part II makes the case for historical and contemporary African American women leaders as important sources for knowledge about leadership. Drawing upon the social text and performance perspectives on discourse and organizing, I illuminate two historical and contemporary discourses about African American women and work—produced in the era of slavery through the postwar and Civil Rights eras to contemporary times—that devalue African American women and that function to silence their potential contributions to the production of leadership knowledge. These discursive texts in historical sequence are: (a) Black women as fallen womanhood/Black women as "natural" laborers, and (b) Black women as marginal workers. In presenting each of these discursive texts, I demonstrate how resistance to these discourses informs a tradition of leadership from the standpoints of African American women that is an exemplar of a meaning centered approach to leadership.

In chapter 3 I take up the first of these discursive texts, emphasizing that the seeds were planted for the emergence of African American women's tradition of leadership through their experiences as workers, community organizers, and Black feminist orators during the era of U.S.-institutionalized slavery.

In chapter 4, I discuss the second discursive text, arguing that in the 100 years after legal emancipation, especially during the years of the Civil Rights Movement, a tradition of African American women's leadership began to take shape as an approach that is applicable to contexts of multicultural change and fragmentation, such as 21st-century organizations.

Part III presents the approach to leadership conceptualized from the standpoints of the African American women executives who participated in this study and exemplary of traditions of African American women's leadership in a contemporary context. This section represents the culmination of the major themes of the book, emphasizing how a tradition of African American women's leadership emerges from a particular way of viewing complex, often contradictory, experiences. The approach is presented as an exemplar of meaning-centered leadership well suited to the increasingly fragmented, multicultural and fundamentally raced, gendered, and classed context of the postindustrial workplace. Specifically, this approach disrupts traditional notions of masculine and feminine leadership and revisions the dichotomous notions of instrumentality versus collaboration and control versus empowerment.

Chapter 5 presents an overview of the leadership themes derived from the study of 15 African American women executives and their co-workers and show how they disrupt traditional masculine and feminine models. It presents a re-envisioning of the traditional notions of instrumental and collaborative leadership in diverse and ambiguous organizational contexts. From the perspectives of the African American women executives in this study, and reminiscent of traditions in African American women's history, collaboration is worked out at the intersections of control and empowerment, where control is (re)defined as interactive and personal, rather than as competitive and distant, and viewed as a necessary approach to leadership within diverse and ambiguous organizational contexts.

In chapter 6 I discuss the themes in more detail, including the voices of the executives and their co-workers. Focusing on the duality of control and empowerment, I show how leadership is revealed as a process of emancipation and change, emphasizing the mutual influence of both leaders and followers in a flow of contested and negotiated meaning production.

In the final chapter, I discuss the implications of this research for developing more inclusive frameworks for researching and conceptualizing leadership in postindustrial organizations. Focusing on the central issues raised in this book—seeking diverse sources of leadership knowledge, foregrounding best practices from multicultural leadership traditions, and re-envisioning 21st-century leadership as meaning centered—I discuss some of the ways in which researchers and practitioners can create multicultural perspectives on leadership and improve our understanding of leadership in the 21st century.

ENDNOTES

1. The leadership approach described in this book was first formulated in the author's dissertation completed at the University of Texas (1997) and later developed further in an article published in *Management Communication Quarterly* (Parker, 2001).
2. I capitalize the terms *Black* and *White* to emphasize the point that race structures the experiences of both groups, but in different ways. "Both racial privilege and racial oppression create categories of people with unique historical experiences that significantly shape their gender identity and attitudes" (Dugger, 1991, p. 57).
3. I use the popular term *African American* to refer to women of African descent that work in dominant U.S.-culture organizations. It is important to acknowledge, however, that some African American women, including myself, find special resonance in using the term *Black* instead of African American, for it can in some ways function as a personal affirmation of Black cultural identity (see Mathis, 2002, pp. 185–187). Also, I acknowledge that the term *African American* refers to a large category of people, including women in the United States who are of African descent, but who define themselves according to their country of origin (e.g., Jamaican American).

4. A recent exception is the inclusion of Lea Williams's (2002) essay on civil rights activist Fannie Lou Hammer in Spears and Lawrence's edited volume on servant leadership. Yet, given the conceptualization of servant leadership as emerging from "a
   deep desire to help others," (Greenleaf, 1977), and the historical portrayal of Black
   women as domestic servants, one might argue that this is not the most progressive
   approach to affirming African American women's leadership, especially given their
   conspicuous absence from other mainstream texts on leadership.

I

The Need for Race- and Gender-Inclusive Visions of Leadership in the Postindustrial Era

Part I of this book brings to the foreground issues of race and gender that are suppressed or neutralized in predominant visions of leadership in both the traditional literature and feminist approaches. The central argument is that problems associated with race neutral theorizing—domination, exclusion, and containment of non-privileged groups—are revealed in the more generalized problems of structural functionalism that produce views of leadership as "good management" and reinforce a traditionally (White, middle-class, heterosexual) masculine model as the symbolic ideal for leadership practice. At the same time, popularized feminist critiques of the gender exclusive masculine leadership model reinforce a White middle class feminine ideal that paradoxically excludes the leadership experiences of women of different races and class statuses.

A fundamental goal of Part I is to show how the silencing of some groups of women and men while privileging others in the study of organizational leadership is a product of the theoretical perspectives that frame our understanding of race, gender, discourse, and organization. In the following chapters I present a review and critique of both the traditional and feminist leadership approaches, propose an inclusive critical feminist framework for studying race, gender, and leadership, and present a meaning centered leadership approach that accommodates a more complex understanding of the leadership processes.

Chapter 1 discusses how the focus on management (as opposed to leadership) in the industrial paradigm has advanced particular race-neutral visions of leadership that are ultimately grounded in traditionally defined White middle class male values and experiences, but that are presented as generalized to all people. This is followed by a critique of popular feminist views of leadership in which the prevailing vision reinforces symbolic images of White, middle-class American women, in effect silencing women of different ethnicities, races, and class statuses, and ultimately reifying a feminine/masculine dichotomy. I use critical communication and feminist perspectives to envision leadership that goes beyond the view of "leadership-as-good-management" that pervades the mainstream literature (Rost, 1991). As will be shown, a critical feminist perspective directs attention away from structural-functionalist views and toward the constitutive processes of leadership (e.g., how leaders and followers do leadership) that occur within raced and gendered organizing contexts.

The chapter concludes with the proposed inclusive feminist framework for envisioning race, gender and leadership. I draw upon Ashcraft's (in press) framing of gender, discourse, and organizing scholarship—gender as socialized and stable (outcome perspective), constantly negotiated (performance perspective), constituted through relations of control (dialectic), or as possible subjectivities, relations, and practices that are embedded in social texts (social text)—that differently attend to issues of race, gender, discourse, and organizing. Such a blending of perspectives is useful in deconstructing the idealized images of a White female and male ideal in leadership theory and practice and reconstructing a more inclusive view of feminine/masculine leadership.

This sets up the discussion in chapter 2, which demonstrates how a meaning centered approach shifts the focus to the leadership process as localized, negotiated and socially constructed, and embraces a both/and orientation that goes beyond rigid dualities such as masculine vs. feminine leadership styles. I use the critical feminist framework developed in the previous chapter, to advance a meaning-centered view of leadership communication that would accommodate the multicultural, racialized, and contradictory viewpoints and paradoxical situational challenges of 21st century organization.

1

Visions of Leadership in Traditional (White Masculine) and (White) Feminine Leadership Approaches: A Review and Critique

[In the study of organizations] The prefix "[W]hite" is usually suppressed, and it is only other racial groups to which we attach prefixes.

—Nkomo (1992, p. 491)

The mainstream literature has produced two competing models of leadership, based almost exclusively on studies of White women and men. However they are presented as race neutral and assumed generalized to all people (Parker & ogilvie, 1996). This chapter presents a review and critique of the predominant visions of leadership based on these models and advances an inclusive critical feminist framework for studying race, gender, and leadership. Critical communication and feminist perspectives distinguish leadership from the view of leadership as "good management" that pervades the mainstream literature (Rost, 1991). Also, it directs attention away from structural-functionalist views toward the constitutive processes of leadership (e.g., how leaders and followers do leadership) that occur within raced- and gendered-organizing contexts.

One model of leadership, which reinforces an industrial paradigm in the traditional literature, is based on the notion of masculine instrumentality. The other, created as a feminist response to the structural-functionalism of the traditional literature, is based on the notion of feminine collaboration. The race-neutral theorizing underlying each of these models has influenced who gets included in studies about leadership (e.g., women of color have been systematically excluded) and the kinds of questions that are asked about leadership behaviors (e.g., cultural assumptions about feminine and masculine leadership are rarely called into question).

Additionally, traditional and certain feminist approaches set up particular ways for envisioning leadership communication that are less well-suited to meeting the challenges of 21st-century organizations. The traditional approach reflects a two-fold problem that emerges from structural-functionalist industrial views of leadership. The problems are conceptualizing leadership as (a) good management (Rost, 1991), and (b) ultimately, traditionally masculine (Barge, 1994; Fine & Buzzanell, 2001; Marshall, 1993; Rost, 1991; Trethewey, 2000). Feminist approaches critique the structural functionalism of the traditional paradigm to include women's leadership experiences. However, the more prominent ones paradoxically exclude potentially valuable sources of leadership knowledge, such as the experiences of African American women, by essentializing the category *woman*. Yet as shown later, when combined in productive ways, feminist perspectives provide a way of envisioning race, gender, and leadership in 21st-century organizations.

VISIONS OF LEADERSHIP COMMUNICATION IN THE INDUSTRIAL PARADIGM: ODE TO THE GREAT (WHITE) MAN

Our mythology refuses to catch up with our reality. We cling to the myth of the Lone Ranger, the romantic idea that great things are usually accomplished by a larger-than-life individual working alone. (Bennis & Biederman, 1996, p. 2)

In the mainstream literature on leadership theory and research[1] the predominant vision of leadership is the Great Man—the triumphant individual taking charge and directing from a distance—in the tradition of White, middle-class constructions of rugged individualism (Bennis & Biederman, 1997; Manz & Sims, 1989; Rost, 1991). This view epitomizes the industrial vision of leadership, advancing the two problematic ideas about leadership earlier mentioned. The fundamental problem is the view of leadership as good management, for it precludes views of leadership as distinct from management and limits an understanding of communication as constitutive of leadership process. It reinforces dualistic thinking about leadership, with an emphasis on individualistic (vs. collective), monologic (vs. dialogic) and transmission (vs. meaning centered) perspectives (Fairhurst, 2001). Furthermore, it reproduces a mythology grounded in the industrial paradigm that infuses the second problem, a traditionally masculine understanding of leadership that, in turn helps to normalize a race-neutral feminine–masculine dualism.

Leadership as "Good Management"

In his comprehensive critique, Rost (1991) emphasized that "leadership-as-good management" *is* the 20th-century's paradigm, and notes that "this understanding of leadership makes perfect sense in an industrial economy" (p. 94). It is a vision of leadership embedded in the structural functionalism of Western culture that is "rational, management oriented, male, technocratic, quantitative, goal dominated, cost-benefit driven, personalistic, hierarchical, short term, pragmatic, and materialistic" (p. 94). In this view, the collective body of leadership theory and research in the past century, which purports to distinguish among traits, styles, and contingency approaches,[2] can effectively be summed up as, "Great men and women with certain preferred traits influencing followers to do what the leaders wish in order to achieve group/organizational goals that reflect excellence defined as some kind of higher-level effectiveness" (p. 180). Rost added that expressive characteristics, such as consideration and other aspects of humanism "boil down to a therapeutic, expressive individualism … [that] help enculturate women into what is essentially a male model of leadership" (p. 94).

The leadership-as-good-management view sets up two problematic issues that have implications for leadership in the complex and ambiguous context of 21st-century organization. First, this view emphasizes the preeminence of the profession of management rather than advancing an understanding of the process of leadership as distinct from management. Management processes can be distinguished from leadership in that the former implies maintaining order through the coordinated actions of people in organizationally established authority relationships, whereas the latter implies intending change through mutually negotiated influence relationships (Jacobs, 1970; Katz & Kahn, 1966/1978; Rost, 1991). A focus on leadership as distinct from management is critical in the postindustrial era of rapid change and globalization, where identities and relationships are not fixed but must be negotiated (Fairclough, 1992). As shown in chapter 3, scholars using meaning centered approaches tend to focus on leadership as opposed to management and, therefore, provide an important frame for studying postindustrial organizational leadership.

The second problem with the leadership-as-good-management view is that it promotes an individualistic, goal-oriented approach to leadership study. Such a view shifts attention away from an understanding of leadership as a negotiated and emergent process. Fairhurst's (2001) critique of the traditional leadership literature reinforces Rost's (1991) claim of an overly individualistic focus and points to important implications for the study of leadership communication. Fairhurst identified the individual-system dichotomy as central among several dualisms in leadership communication research that highlight the paradoxical nature of leadership theory, research, and practice. She noted, as Rost did, that historically, the predominant views of leadership have been influenced by a psychological view of the world where "in a figure-ground arrangement the individual is figure and communication is incidental or, at best, intervening" (Fairhurst, 2001, p. 383). Related secondary dualisms exist in the form of transmission versus meaning-centered views of communication and cognitive outcomes versus conversational practices. The focus on message transmission and cognitive outcomes (e.g., individualistic focus on leadership traits, cognitions, acts, and one-way meaning construction) has dominated the leadership literature (Fairhurst, 2001), and contributes to romanticizing the perceived role of the leader (Meindl, Ehrlich, & Dukerich, 1985).

However, increasingly, scholars are emphasizing a systems orientation that reconceptualizes leadership as an emergent property of group interaction (see Fisher, 1985, 1986), exchanges between leaders and group members (Dansereau, 1995a, 1995b; Jablin, Miller, & Keller, 1999), a dialogue (Isaacs, 1993, 1999), or as distributed among leaders and followers that are empowered to bring about organizational transformation (Conger, 1989; Kouzes & Posner, 1995, 1995; Senge, 1990; Senge et al., 1999; Wheatley, 1992). A systems orientation directs attention to meaning-centered views of leadership communication and the relational and conversational practices associated with doing leadership.

Yet, rather than simply shifting from an individualistic to a systems orientation, Fairhurst (2001) advocated using "both/and" thinking about key dualisms and paradoxes in leadership research. Either/or thinking usually causes researchers to favor one view over another, and over time, produces dominant versus marginal perspectives, such as the race-neutral bias mentioned earlier, and the individualistic orientation of the leadership communication literature. A both/and approach allows researchers to see the wider systems concerns and individual concerns, and to view communication more complexly, as transmission and meaning centered and studied as both cognitive outcomes and conversational practices. That is, Fairhurst aptly demonstrated that it is important to highlight the tensions that emerge from the individual-systems dialectic and other dualisms, treating these as problematic and focusing on how the tensions themselves are managed.

As shown in the next chapter, critical interpretive meaning-centered approaches to leadership provide a both/and frame that foregrounds the tensions of negotiating relationships and identities within the complex multicultural, raced and gendered communicative context of 21st-century organization. First, however, is a discussion of the second problem emerging from the industrial paradigm, an understanding of leadership communication as essentially masculine and reifying the feminine–masculine dichotomy.

Normalizing the Feminine–Masculine Dichotomy: Leadership Communication as Traditionally Masculine

Focusing on leadership as good management ultimately reinforces a masculine model of leadership communication, inasmuch as management processes have been defined in traditionally masculine terms, such as authority, structure, and instrumentality. As conceptualized in the leadership literature, the masculine model emphasizes a hierarchical approach in which leaders initiate structure while demonstrating autonomy, strength, self-efficacy, and control (Bem, 1974; Eagly, 1987; Loden, 1985). This model is representative of "male values" (Marshall, 1993) and is most associated with traditional understandings of men's socialized communication patterns (Tannen, 1990; Wood, 1998). According to this perspective, men use more instrumental communication—unilateral, directive and aimed at controlling others—that is consistent with their learned view of talk as a way to assert self and achieve status (Eagly & Karau, 1991). Distance and detachment are common communication themes associated with male values (Marshall, 1993). Common symbolic representations of the masculine leadership model include characteristics such as aggressiveness, independence, risk-taking, rationality, and intelligence (Collins, 1998b; Connell, 1995).

A traditionally masculine model of leadership communication pervades the mainstream leadership literature (Alvesson & Billing, 1997; Buzzanell, Ellingson, Silvio, Pasch, Dale, Mauro, Smith, Weir, & Martin, 2002; Fine & Buzzanell, 2000; Parker, 2001; Rost, 1991). Rost provided one of the most comprehensive critiques of this literature and, among other things, observes that this literature reinforces a male model of life. Fine and Buzzanell reviewed mainstream approaches to leadership that focusing on serving, including adaptive leadership (Heifetz, 1994; Heifetz & Laurie, 1997; transformational leadership (Burns, 1978), and self and Superleadership (Sims & Manz, 1996). They concluded that these approaches are essentially "'manstories' (Gergen, 1990; Marshall, 1989) [for] they involve often solitary searches for fulfillment and use service to others as a means of developing followers who can assist in achieving organizational or societal goals" (p. 143).

Even so-called "alternative" approaches, such as servant leadership (Greenleaf, 1977) and some "feminine perspectives" are either primarily male centered or they implicitly reinforce traditional understandings of men's socialized communication patterns and worldview (Fine & Buzzannell, 2001, 143). For example, Fine and Buzzanell noted that in describing servant leadership as an alternative to traditional approaches, Greenleaf "universalizes the experience of seeker, maintains organizational structures, and never questions the ways in which gender relations may make servant leadership a very different process for women and for men" (Fine & Buzzanell, p. 143).

Furthermore, some feminist perspectives implicitly reinforce a traditionally masculine view and, some would argue, are being co-opted by masculinist aims (Aschcraft, in press). Feminist critiques of the structural-functionalism of the industrial paradigm expose an alternative vision of leadership communication aimed at valorizing "feminine" leadership as having a relationship rather than an instrumental orientation (Helgesen, 1990, Lunneborg, 1990; Rosener, 1990). However, even in feminine leadership, instrumental outcomes primarily determine the effectiveness and usefulness of the leadership style (Calàs 1993; Fine & Buzzanell, 2001; Fletcher, 1994). Moreover, some scholars have argued persuasively that contemporary organizations standardize feminization while maintaining a gender-neutral stance (Ashcraft, in press; Fondas, 1997; May, 1997).

Notwithstanding the view that feminist leadership approaches implicitly reinforce a masculine view as the ultimate measure of effectiveness, the claims of valorizing feminine leadership as an alternative to masculine leadership explicitly reinforce a feminine–masculine dualism. That is, they portray feminine leadership as being in opposition to masculine leadership. However, these approaches do not acknowledge the diversity among women's (or men's) experiences that shape leadership knowledge, and the possibilities of feminine–masculine duality (e.g., a both/and approach). Though not grounded in the implicit image of the Great White Man, as is the industrial model, the predominant vision of feminine leadership is implicitly based on an ideal White Woman.

(WHITE) FEMININE VISIONS OF LEADERSHIP

Feminist perspectives critique the persistence of male dominance in social arrangements and advocate some form of change to the status quo (Calàs & Smirich, 1996). However, despite the common focus on critique and change, there are a range of feminist approaches—liberal, radical, psychoanalytic,

Marxist, socialist, poststructuralist and postmodern, and postcolonial—that vary in their ontology, epistemological positions and degree of political critique, and therefore vary in the type of influence on leadership theory. Feminist visions of change range from "'reforming' organizations; to 'transforming' organizations *and* society; to transforming our prior understandings of what constitutes knowledge/theory/practice" (Calàs & Smircich, 1996, p. 219).

Overview of Feminist Approaches

Feminist approaches to leadership communication are part of the voluminous literature on "women in management" that began to accumulate in the late-1960s and early-1970s when the number of White middle-class women in management (and to a lesser extent women and men of color) began to increase. These approaches range from the liberal feminist views of the 1960s and 1970s that advocated women emulate the masculine language of management, to the more recent radical, psychoanalytic, and socialist views that advance alternative feminist leadership approaches (albeit from different epistemological stances), to poststructuralist and postmodern feminisms that deconstruct essentialist views of leadership as feminine and masculine.

Universalizing the "Feminine"

As discussed later, when combined in productive ways, feminist perspectives provide promise for informing a more inclusive and sufficiently complex framework for envisioning leadership in 21st-century organizations. However, I argue that the prevailing vision of feminist leadership is one that reinforces symbolic images of White, middle-class American women, which in effect, silences women of different ethnicities, races, and class statuses. The so-called "female advantage" approach to leadership emerging from radical and psychoanalytic feminisms, argues that a "distinctly feminine" style of leadership makes women better leaders than men (Helgesen, 1990, Lunneborg, 1990; Rosener, 1990). According to this view, feminine leadership, is an outcome of girls' and women's sex role socialization that produces passive, nurturing, relationship-oriented leaders. This view is in stark contrast to men's socialized leadership—aggressive, rational, strong, independent leaders (Helgesen, 1990; Loden, 1985; Rosener, 1990). The central argument, however, is that the feminine style, grounded in female values such as relationship-building, interdependence and being other-focused, is better suited than the male hierarchical approach to leading contemporary complex organizing contexts, but it is stifled by current, male-dominated structuring that values hierarchy, independence, and self-efficacy processes (Grossman & Chester, 1990; Helgesen, 1990; Lunneborg, 1990).

The view of feminine leadership as distinct from a masculine approach is advanced in organizational studies as well as in the popular literature on leadership—books and articles written by management consultants and organizational development specialists—contributing to its reification in the popular consciousness. Helgesen's (1990) best-selling volume, *The Feminine Advantage,* is exemplary. In it, she described what she called the "feminine principles of management" which are characterized as principles of caring, making intuitive decisions, and viewing leadership from a nonhierarchical perspective. Helgesen argued that whereas male-dominated organizations are almost always hierarchical, women tend to think of organization in terms of a network or web of relationships, with leadership at the center of the web, not at the top of a pyramid.

The female advantage argument provides an important critique of the patriarchal discourses that exclude women's experiences. However, it is problematic because it is presented as a race-neutral, universal representation of all women, based on the socialized experiences of middle-class White women (Parker & olgivie, 1996). Most importantly, it fails to acknowledge that notions of feminine and masculine are social, cultural, and historical products, constructed according to racial and sexual ideologies that conscript women's and men's embodied identities (Trethewey, 2000). This oversight is significant for the study of African American women leaders given that socially constructed images of White women historically have been used in the systematic oppression of Black women (Morton, 1991), a point that is developed more fully in chapter 3. To advance a model of feminine leadership based on White women's gender identity essentially excludes Black women's experiences in constructing gender identity and therefore excludes Black women's voices in theorizing about leadership.

Thus, in an attempt to raise the voices of women in leadership, the feminine advantage model contributes to the silencing of marginalized groups, including, but not limited to, Black women. The feminine advantage model does not critique the controlling images of woman as the enabling helpmate and man as the assertive status seeker. Instead, in many ways, it works to reify patriarchal authority and perpetuate distortions of women and men as "feminine" or "masculine."[3] In leadership theory, these images usually form around the dichotomized notions of men as masculine leaders—aggressive, rational, strong, independent leaders—and women as feminine leaders—passive, nurturing, relationship-oriented leaders (Helgesen, 1990; Loden, 1985; Rosener, 1990).

GENDERED LEADERSHIP COMMUNICATION
AND THE PROBLEMS OF RACE-NEUTRAL THEORIZING

Both the feminine advantage model and the leadership-as-good-management model of the industrial paradigm reinforce the three problems of race-neutral theorizing identified in the Introduction—domination, exclusion, and containment. It reinforces Western- (White middle and upper class) gendered identities as the ideal, and in upholding that ideal, it at once excludes the experiences of other groups and renders them nonlegitimate or peripheral. For example, as race-neutral descriptions of feminine and masculine leadership are treated as universal gender symbols, as they often are within dominant culture institutions (Collins, 1998b), African American women's experiences are excluded or distorted, as are the experiences of other women of color, men of color, and nonmiddle-class White women and men. Patricia Hill Collins (1998b) made this point when she said that:

> Aggressive Black and Hispanic men are seen as dangerous, not powerful, and are often penalized when they exhibit any of the allegedly "masculine" characteristics. Working class and poor White men fare slightly better and are also denied the allegedly "masculine" symbols of leadership, intellectual competence, and human rationality. Women of color and working class and poor White women are also not represented [by universal gender symbolism], for they have never had the luxury of being "ladies." (pp. 217–218)

Warren and Bourque (1991) made a similar point in their critique of approaches to "feminizing" technology and strategies for intervention in developing countries. As summarized by Calàs and Smircich (1996), these researchers warn against a universal "natural woman(ness)" that is a product of the Western ideal of the egalitarian, nonviolent, and nurturing woman:

> This perspective dangerously romanticizes women's values, the family, the separation of "domestic" and "public" spheres, and the nature of Third World societies, the negotiation of gender identities as they are realized in practice, and the interplay of family dynamics and legal systems to challenge these images of male and female. (Warren & Borque, 1991, p. 287, quoted in Calàs & Smircich, 1996, p. 241)

The silencing of some groups of women and men while privileging others in the study of organizational leadership is a product of the theoretical perspectives that frame our understanding of gender, discourse, and organization. In the next section, I advance an inclusive theoretical framework for understanding gender, race, and leadership that deconstructs Western (White, middle and upper class) representations of the masculine–feminine dualism and reconstructs new complex understandings of leadership processes.

AN INCLUSIVE CRITICAL FEMINIST FRAMEWORK
FOR CONCEPTUALIZING LEADERSHIP
COMMUNICATION

If we are to develop an inclusive feminist framework for understanding organizational leadership in a global, post-industrial context, we must call into question the dichotomized race-neutral notions of "feminine" and "masculine," portrayed in the traditional masculine and "feminine advantage" models of organizational leadership, as well as other dualisms in the leadership literature (Fairhurst, 2001). This calls for multi-faceted frameworks that deconstruct the claims of discourses that lock subjects into fixed raced and gendered identities and focus attention on the fluidity, contradictions, paradoxes and tensions of organizational life.

Ashcraft (in press) offers a useful frame, based on the relationships among discourse, gender, and organization, that informs a more complex and inclusive feminist framework for conceptualizing leadership communication, and that implicitly reveals the influence of the various feminist perspectives. Using Ashcraft's structure, I advance an inclusive feminist framework that blends perspectives in ways that destabilize the normative claims of the feminine/masculine dichotomy and revision organizational leadership more complexly.

Gender, Discourse, and Organization: Blending
Perspectives to Advance Complexity and Inclusivity

Ashcraft (in press) identifies four perspectives that conveniently frame the gender and organization literature to reveal the relative complexity and inclusiveness that scholars have incorporated into the study of gendered organizational processes, including leadership. Her framing of this literature also implicitly reveals the influence of the various feminist perspectives that differently attend to multiple systems of oppression such as race, class, and gender. Focusing on the relative emphasis on "micro," "meso" and "macro" dimensions of discourse in gender and organizational scholarship, Ashcraft asserts that gender is viewed alternatively as (a) socialized and stable (outcome perspective), (b) constantly negotiated (performance perspective), (c) constituted through relations of control (dialectic perspective), or (d) as possible subjectivities, relations, and practices that are embedded in social texts (social text perspective).

In the first perspective, discourse is an effect or outcome, emphasizing how gender identity shapes organizational communication choices such as leadership and managing conflict. This view of gender and discourse is reflected in the feminine advantage model. In the remaining three perspectives discourse is seen as constitutive (though in different ways, as discussed later) highlighting how discursive activity continuously creates, solidifies, disrupts, and alters gendered selves and organizational forms (Ashcraft, in press). Championing one frame (e.g., the outcome perspective of the feminine advantage model) inevitably leads to exclusionary thinking. As Ashcraft correctly notes, "each frame generates moments of 'truth' about gendered organization, which also obscures alternating and simultaneous truths" (in press). Needed are multi-faceted frameworks that "blend ways of seeing and so, blur the needless boundaries between them" (Ashcraft, in press).

Here, I advance an inclusive feminist framework that combines aspects of the social text, performance, and dialectic, perspectives of gender, discourse and organizing. This framework reflects a confluence of radical, socialist, and poststructuralist feminist perspectives that help to destabilize the normative claims of the feminine advantage leadership model and to revision gender and organizational leadership more complexly. Specifically, the blending of perspectives addresses the problems emerging from the feminine/masculine dualism, such as race-neutral views of gendered leadership. Also, it enables a both/and approach to leadership process that moves beyond the individual/collective, transmission/meaning centered/ and conversation/text dualisms.

Destabilizing the Feminine/Masculine Dualism in Leadership

Combining aspects of the performance and social text approaches to gendered discourse provides a framework for disrupting the White feminine ideal of leadership and destabilizing the feminine/masculine dualism. The performance perspective posits a dialectical relation between two levels of discourse—mundane interaction and the larger social texts that are "temporarily fixed (but never determined), relatively coherent (though also conflicted), context-specific 'script,' or symbolic abstraction, that guides situated performances" (Ashcraft, in press). However, emphasis is placed on performance in mundane interaction where "social actors' talk is always 'positioning' self and other in terms of available gender narratives, which facilitate and delimit possibilities for action" (Goffman, 1976, 1977; Ashcraft, in press).

A performance frame is useful for it points to gender as a discursive accomplishment, and it reflects socialist feminisms' attention to intersectionality as a guiding principle for analysis. Socialist feminists see gender as "processual and socially constituted through several intersections of sex, race, ideology, and experiences of oppression under patriarchy and capitalism (that are distinct systems)" (Calàs and Smircich, 1996, p. 220). Thus, rather than being a stable outcome, as portrayed in the feminine advantage model of leadership, the performance frame conceptualizes gendered identity as a partial, unstable discursive effect that is (re)produced in the dynamic tension between everyday interaction and normative expectations about gender behavior.

However, the focus on interaction in the performance frame tends to downplay the political and ideological systems of power relations that influence organizational performances (Collins, 2002). This is where a social text frame, in concert with the performance view, becomes most useful in deconstructing the idealized images of a White female and male ideal in leadership theory and practice and reconstructing a more inclusive view of feminine/masculine leadership. A social text perspective views discourse as "a broader societal narrative embedded in systems of representation, which offer predictable yet elastic, lucid yet contradictory images of possible subjectivities, relations among them, and attendant disciplinary practices (Bederman, 1995; Connell, 1995; Mouffe, 1995)" (Ashcraft, in press). Rather than focusing on "communication *in* or *of* organization," attention shifts to "communication *about* organization or how society portrays and debates its institutions and the very notion of work" (Ashcraft, in press).

The social text perspective reflects the postmodern/poststructuralist feminist stance on the discursive nature of "social reality" and "subjectivity." In poststructuralist feminisms, "sex/gender are discursive practices that constitute specific subjectivities through power and resistance in the materiality of human bodies" (Calàs & Smircich, 1996, p. 221). This requires "ongoing deconstruction and denaturalization of discourses and practices that constitute it" (Calàs & Smircich, p. 221).

Thus, converse to the performance bias toward interaction, the emphasis in the social text perspective shifts to the generative nature of larger social texts, drawn from representations in popular culture and other sources, such as film, literature, and scholarship. This shift allows a deconstruction and denaturalization of discourses and practices that (re)constitute the Western dominant cultural ideals of the feminine and masculine in organizational processes, such as leadership. As Mumby and Putnam (1992) note, the deconstruction move "challenges commonsense understanding of gender and taken-for-granted definitions of masculine and feminine" (p. 467). One way in which researchers have already moved forward in the deconstruction project is to expose the privileging and reproduction of dominant cultural ideologies about gender in organizational studies (cf., Calàs & Smircich, 1991; Mumby & Putnam, 1992). However, these studies generally critique masculinity, without calling into question the hegemony of Western ideals of femininity.

Combining the performance and social text perspectives allows for an emphasis on *both* human agency *and* social deconstruction. Standpoint feminisms provide the epistemological tools for such a combination of perspectives.

Standpoint Feminisms: A Both/and Approach.   Feminist standpoint theories (Collins,1990, 1998a; Haraway, 1997; Harding, 1991, 1996; Hartsock, 1987; Smith, 1987), particularly those that explore connections between socially located standpoints and postmodernism (see Harding, 1996; Hirschmann, 1997; O'Brien Hallstein, 1997), provide the epistemological tools for applying performance and social text perspectives on gender, discourse, and leadership communication. Feminist standpoint theorists argue that women as a group occupy a distinct position and potential standpoint in culture because, "under the sexual division of labor ensconced in patriarchy, women have been systematically exploited, oppressed, excluded, devalued, and dominated" (O'Brien Hallstein, 2000, p. 5).

Although earlier work using standpoint theory emphasized women's common experiences, current work recognizes that women's common experience is different among groups to the extent that material experience differs. For example, standpoint theorists using poststructural approaches call attention to the pluralities of power relations and other historical cultural forces "that are disseminated through 'discourses' that are both structural and symbolic" (Harding, 1996, p. 451). That is, the interlocking systems of oppression such as race, class, and gender create the potential for different standpoints among women (Collins, 1990, 2002; Harding, 1991; 1996).[4]

Standpoints, according to Haraway (1997), are "cognitive-emotional-political achievements, crafted out of located social-historical-bodily experience— itself always constituted through fraught, noninnocent, discursive, material collective practices" (p. 304, n.32). From this perspective, a standpoint is more than simply occupying a particular societal position from which to stage performances. Standpoints are achieved through

> active, political resistance to work against the material embodiment of the perspective and experience of the dominant group. It is the act of having to push against the experience-made-reality of the hegemonic group that makes it a political standpoint and potentially liberating. (Welton, 1997, p.11).[5]

A fundamental tenet of standpoint epistemology is that the standpoints of women and others marginalized by intersecting systems of oppression (i.e., race, class, gender, age, and sexual orientation), emerge from positions from which they are able to see, not only their own positions, but the dominant system as a whole. This view from the margins is often referred to as the "outsider within" perspective (Collins 1990, 1998a). Outsiders within the dominant culture are assumed to be able to provide a more complete and less distorting social perspective (Harding, 1987) than is possible from the point of view of the "insiders" or more privileged group members (usually White, middle-class men). Collins (1990) theorized that the dimensions of Black women's stand-points are: (a) the presence of characteristic core themes, such as a enduring a legacy of struggle, rejecting racist images, and creating self definitions (Lubiano, 1992); (b) the diversity of Black women's experiences in encountering these core themes; (c) the varying expressions of Black women's Afrocentric feminist consciousness regarding the core themes and their experiences with them; and (d) the interdependence of Black women's experiences, consciousness, and actions. This view of Black women's standpoints is consistent with the focus on both performance and social text as discursive frames, in its emphasis on individual women negotiating and resisting raced and gendered identities in light of dominant cultural texts that affirm their collective social location.

Two important goals of standpoint epistemology are to center the experiences of women and others marginalized by dominant culture, and to create positive social change (Dougherty & Krone, 2000). Centering the experiences of women, such as African American women, whose experiences challenge the Western ideals of femininity is an important way to disrupt traditional notions of feminine and masculine leadership. In the current global context, the idealized images of leaders fitting the stereotype of Western (middle-class White) womanhood and manhood are reinforced and popularized in literature and in the media. Meanwhile, other groups, such as African American women, are cast in literature, media, and societal practices through negative stereotypes that do not fit the idealized Western images. We can begin to see the overlap in discourse-as-social text and discourse- as-performance, as "people consume these representations, drawing upon and/or resisting them in the performances of everyday organizational life" (Ashcraft, in press).

Taken together, the performance and social text frames provide a way of conceptualizing leadership interaction as a site for negotiating and resisting raced and gendered identities in light of dominant cultural expectations for "appropriate" leader, gender, and race behavior. Rather than envisioning feminine or masculine leadership that conjures up images of a fixed subject, we can imagine leadership in terms of multiple subjectivities that are (re)produced and resisted in interaction. Such a view positions leadership interaction both as product and producer of gendered and raced identities, and a site for deconstructing the universal race-neutral symbols of masculine and feminine leadership.

This suggests that leadership theorists should seek ways "to disrupt ongoing discourses fixing human identities and social relations in 'men' and 'women,' [and I would add, in fixed racial categories] thereby weakening the impact of this organizing principle" (Alvesson & Billing, 1997, p. 219). One way of doing so is to examine the ways in which leaders and followers, in their everyday interactions, (re)produce, resist, and redefine meanings of gender and race as organizing principles. Such a focus benefits from a third perspective on gender and discourse, the dialectical frame.

Foregrounding Tensions and Paradoxes in Leadership Processes

A third, and in some ways mediating, frame useful for reconceptualizing leadership as an inclusive construct, is the dialectic perspective. The dialectic frame points to the tensions between organizing (e.g., performance and conversation) and organization (e.g., social text). Also, the dialectic frame attends to the tensions that emerge from the individual-systems dualism in leadership theory. The focus shifts to a both/and frame, treating these dualisms as problematic and focusing on how the tensions themselves are managed.

In the dialectic frame, organization can be seen as a cultural artifact (Prasad, 1997) of the larger social text—the interlocking systems of oppression, such as race, gender, and class, that structure organization (Acker, 1990). This focuses attention on organizations as fundamentally raced, gendered, and classed structures (Parker, 2003). In dynamic tension with raced, gendered and classed organization systems are the ongoing conversations that reveal the paradoxical situations of everyday organizational life. Thus a blending of the performance, dialectic, and social text perspectives highlights the interplay between performance and conversation (e.g., individual concerns) and social text (system concerns). From this perspective, it is possible to foreground the hidden tensions, racial and gender conflicts, and paradoxes of organizational life.

Prasad (1997) argued that organizational systems themselves are cultural artifacts influenced by larger social texts—especially myths and other cultural narratives that shape organizational rules, values, taboos, and practices.[6] She used the term *cultural imprinting* following Stinchcombe (1965), to show how certain social and cultural preferences become reflected or imprinted in an organization's formal and informal functioning, and then become taken for granted as they are institutionalized in the organization's routine structure. She argued that cultural imprints of the industrial paradigm, left by the Protestant work ethic and the myths of the frontier, define contemporary notions of the "ideal employee" and "who fits accepted modes of organizational practice and who does not" (Prasad, 1996, p. 140). She theorized that cultural tensions in organizing are "produced as a result of the cultural clashes between cultural codes governing various societal subcultures on the one hand, and the dominant cultural codes of contemporary organizations on the other" (p. 143).

Focusing on the cultural tensions produced in organizing makes it evident that gender and race are not neutral elements, but are constitutive of organizing and are primary ways of signifying power in social systems (Acker, 1991; Scott, 1986). Thus theorizing about leadership and other processes should focus on the hidden microprocesses and micropractices (e.g., conversation and performances) that produce and reproduce unequal, and persistent, sex-, race-, and class-based organizational structures (organization). At the same time, attention should be paid to "discursive strategies through which members manage such tensions, as well as the larger discourses of organizing their tactics imply" (Ashcraft, in press)

From this perspective, the site of organizational leadership—routine mundane practices such as decision making, coordinating work processes, client interaction, as well as other operational practices such as recruitment, hiring, placement, promotions—are sites where conflicting cultural narratives and shifting subjectivities are negotiated (Parker, 2003). This directs attention to leadership as a process by which organizational members—leaders and followers—struggle to create meaning within such contexts.

SUMMARY

In this chapter, I have shown how both the traditional literature and feminist approaches contribute to a three-fold problem that limits our vision of leadership and excludes potentially valuable sources of leadership knowledge. The traditional leadership literature forms the basis of these problems with (a) its focus on management (as opposed to leadership), (b) advancing ideas that leadership is good management and (b) ultimately grounded in traditionally defined male values. Paradoxically, feminist approaches both contribute to some aspects of these problems, and provide promise for developing more inclusive frameworks. For example feminist approaches critique the emphasis on male values, which reinforce the dualistic notions of feminine and masculine leadership. At the same time, feminist critiques of the structural-functionalism that pervades the traditional literature provides promise for re-envisioning leadership in the postindustrial era. Toward that end, I presented an inclusive feminist framework that combines aspects of the social text, performance, and dialectic, perspectives of gender, discourse and organizing. This framework reflects a confluence of radical, socialist, and poststructuralist feminist perspectives that help to destabilize the normative claims of the feminine advantage leadership model and to revision gender and organizational leadership more complexly. In the next chapter, I use this framework as to advance a meaning-centered approach to leadership.

ENDNOTES

1. For comprehensive reviews of the traditional leadership literature see, Bass (1990) and Yukl (2002).
2. For critical reviews of this literature, see Cheney, Christensen, Zorn, & Ganesh (2004), and Rost (1991).
3. Several other writers (see Ashcraft, in press; Calàs & Smircich, 1993; Ely,1991; Fletcher, 1994; Wood,1994) have noted the potentially dangerous political and social consequences of supporting "uniquely female" contributions to society in general and to organizations in particular. For example, Ely (1991) argued that the emphasis on women as relationship-oriented provides a slippery slope toward support of arguments for the appropriateness of a sexual division of labor. Specifically, such an argument is based on an assumption of women's natural proclivities to spend their time catering to the needs of others, supporting men and a traditional family through altruism and self- sacrifice. Similarly, Wood (1994) argued that "to encourage women to define themselves by their capacities to care and respond to others is to reinforce their traditionally subordinate, tentative positions in society; it also undercuts critical reflection on those roles" (p. 82).
4. Collins (1998a) warned that postmodern and deconstructive approaches may work against Black women's strides toward group authority and therefore group action against oppression. However, she concedes that postmodernism can be a potentially powerful means for challenging "not just the results of dominant discourses, but the rules of the game itself" (p. 154). It seems she suggested that postmodern and deconstructive approaches useful to the extent that they reveal structures of domination:

    It is one thing for African American women and similarly situated groups to use deconstructive methodologies to dismantle hierarchical power relations. However, it is quite another for members of the privileged elites to appropriate these same tools … to undercut the bases of authority of those long excluded from centers of power. (p. 145)

5. For recent interpretive reviews of standpoint theories from communication perspectives, see the 2000 special issue of *Women's Studies in Communication, 23*(1), with the introduction by O'Brien Hallstein (2000).
6. In a related argument Browning (1991) proposed a compelling theory about the narrative structuring of organizational communication through the interplay of *lists* (rooted in the language of science to convey certainty, standards, and accountability) and *stories* (grounded in persuasive cultural narratives to convey a particular course of action).

2

A Meaning-Centered Approach to Leadership in the Postindustrial Era: A Critical Feminist Perspective

The leadership-as-good management view that has dominated the study of leadership communication is too limited for envisioning leadership in the postindustrial era, for it places an emphasis on goals and outcomes, which assumes we can objectively characterize persons (e.g., as masculine and feminine) and situations (as functionally ordered) to achieve those goals and outcomes (Cheney, Christensen, Zorn, & Ganesh, 2004). Although this view may have been effective for doing leadership in the industrial economy, it is too limiting for the rapid change and ambiguity of the postindustrial global economy (Rost, 1991). More fundamentally, it is not well-suited for the multicultural, racialized, often contradictory viewpoints and paradoxical situational challenges of 21st-century organization (Parker, 2001).

In this chapter, I use the critical feminist framework developed in the previous chapter, to advance a meaning-centered view of leadership communication that would theoretically accommodate the complexity of postindustrial organization. I begin with a discussion of communication and postindustrial organizational cultures, as characterized by fragmentation, ambiguity, and difference, highlighting the centrality of race and gender in everyday organizing, and emphasizing the usefulness of critical feminist perspectives for conceptualizing leadership communication. Next is a meaning-centered definition of leadership that emphasizes a localized, negotiated process of mutual influence and change that occurs in dynamic tension with larger cultural texts.

COMMUNICATION AND POSTINDUSTRIAL ORGANIZATION: CONFRONTING ISSUES OF FRAGMENTATION, AMBIGUITY, AND DIFFERENCE

A common way of envisioning contemporary, postindustrial societies is that in which identities and relationships are not fixed but must be negotiated (Fairclough, 1992). This condition emerges in part from globalization in a market economy that is increasingly diverse and multicultural (Cheney et al., 2004). People of both sexes and of different gender identities, ethnicities, races, classes, sexual orientations, and so on, are interacting in ways that help them find meaning and connection in a social world that is increasingly fragmented and disconnected (Giddens, 1991). This view directs attention to postindustrial organizations as fragmented cultures. Cheney et al. (2004) define culture as "a system of meaning that guides the construction of reality in a social community" (p. 76). In organizations cultural meaning systems are constituted in the members' assumptions (e.g., core beliefs), values, (e.g., expressed in behavioral norms), and physical and performative artifacts (e.g., dress and logos; rituals, ceremonies, traditions, and stories [Schein, 1992]).

The fragmentation perspective characterizes organizational cultures as diverse (not unitary or integrated) meaning systems suffused with ambiguity, where consensus and dissensus (e.g., the degree that reality makes sense) are issue specific and constantly fluctuating (Martin, 1992). Communication takes on a particular negotiated character in a fragmented and ambiguous social world in which identities and relationships are not fixed. Fairclough (1995) identified several characteristics of communication in postindustrial societies that underscore the negotiated character of communication in this context. Some of these include an increased demand for highly developed dialogical capacities; social interaction that is more conversational, informal, and democratic; an increase in self-promotional discourse; and more technologically based communication.

A larger cultural text that reproduces and institutionalizes racism and sexism poses particular challenges for developing and facilitating dialogic, conversational, self-promotional, and technologically based communication capacities. I argue, following Essed (1991), that the fundamental social relations of postindustrial society are racialized relations. This suggests that identities, including gendered identities, are negotiated as part of a larger cultural text that reproduces race relations. Essed used the term *subtle gendered racism* to characterize certain types of subtle discrimination that target African American women, and her theory of everyday racism exemplifies this. Using cross-cultural empirical data, Essed (1991) developed a theory of everyday racism, that she defined as:

> a process in which (a) socialized racist notions are integrated into meanings that make practices immediately definable and manageable, (b) practices with racist implications become in themselves familiar and repetitive, and (c) underlying racial and ethnic relations are actualized and reinforced through these routine or familiar practices in everyday situations. (p. 52)

Similarly, critical race theorists point out that racism is "normal, not aberrant, in American society" (Delgado, 1995, p. xiv), and "because it is so enmeshed in the fabric of the U.S. social order, it appears both normal and natural to people in this society" (Ladson-Billings, 2000, p. 264).

In the study of organizational communication, this calls for a shift away from race-neutral understandings of organization and the myopic focus on gender as distinct from a larger cultural text of race relations. Specifically, there should be a move toward reconceptualizing race not as a simple property of individuals but as an integral dynamic of organizations (Nkomo, 1992). As Nkomo aptly noted, this implies a move toward phenomenological and historical research methods that would contribute toward building theories and knowledge about how race is produced and how it is a core feature of organizations. Relevant to the present study, if organizations were viewed as fundamentally raced, then organizational leadership would have to take into account how race relations fundamentally impact everyday interactions within organizations.

Ashcraft and Allen (2003) advocated foregrounding race as central to organizational life. Through their analysis of the racial subtext of organizational communication texts, they demonstrated how the process of reinforcing a particular way of viewing racial relations occurs through theory development in organizational communication, which informs organizational communication practice. They revealed five disciplined messages that "function to sustain raced organization, for they support and obscure the tacit Whiteness of much organizational communication theory" (Ashcraft & Allen, 2003, p. 28).

Conceptualizing postindustrial communication contexts as multicultural and fundamentally raced reinforces the importance of a both/and approach to understanding leadership in terms of individual and systems phenomena. From a critical feminist perspective, leadership can be understood as a socially constructed process of negotiating difference, taking into account the interlocking oppressions of race, gender, and class that structure organizational life. Grounded in this perspective, I advance a meaning-centered leadership approach that takes into account tensions emerging from the individual-systems dualism and that shifts the focus to leadership as a process of change and emancipation.

FOREGROUNDING MEANING-CENTERED APPROACHES TO LEADERSHIP

Meaning-centered approaches reveal leadership as an ongoing process of social construction (Bensen, 1977; Berger & Luckmann, 1966). These approaches reflect a critical interpretive view of reality, where in "the individual takes an active, constructive role in creating knowledge through language and communication" (Fairhurst, 2001, p. 385). Grounded in the symbolic interaction perspective (Blumer, 1969; Mead, 1934), meaning-centered approaches reveal leadership as a symbolic, interactive process through which meaning is created, sustained and changed (Avolio & Bass, 2002; Deetz, 2000; Fairhurst & Sarr, 1996; Parker, 2001; Rost 1991; Smircich & Morgan, 1982). Cheney et al. (2004) favored a socially constructed view of leaders and leadership situations "as being open to multiple meanings, readings, or interpretations" (p. 192).

Much of this research centers on charismatic and visionary leadership. This literature takes a monologic view, focusing on the leader as the creator and manager of symbolic communication (e.g., myths, legends, stories, and rituals) (see, Fairhurst, 2001).

Another line of research shifts to a more systems interactive view. A number of theorists in this line of research advocate studying "alternative" approaches to leadership and organizing (Ashcraft, 2000, 2001; Buzzanell et al., 1994; Putnam & Kolb, 2000). For example, Buzzanell and her colleagues summarized this literature in terms of three alternative rationales for organizing. First are contra-bureaucratic structures that resist organization that promotes "the employer viewpoint," such as universalism. Second are contra-instrumental relationship approaches that resist the devaluation of noninstrumental and nongoal-oriented activities. Third are value-rational or ideologically focused organization approaches that resist societal values that privilege individual, corporate, and competitive ethics. These approaches are exemplary in illuminating the processes that constrain the development of participatory practices in leadership. However they do so by emphasizing the either/or thinking in leadership theory that often suppresses other important elements in the process (Fairhurst, 2001).

This volume adds to the literature advocating alternative leadership approaches. However, in concert with other communication scholars and organizational development theorists (Baxter & Montgomery, 1996; Stohl & Cheney,

2001; Fairhurst, 2001; Senge, 1990), I advocate shifting attention toward more dialogic both/and views of leadership and organizing. This shifts the focus toward understanding the mutual influence of both structure and process. It captures more completely the relationship of leaders and followers in a flow of contested and negotiated meaning production. More specifically, I advance a meaning-centered leadership approach as seen through a critical feminist lens of emancipation and change.

DEFINING LEADERSHIP IN THE POSTINDUSTRIAL ERA

I combine two meaning-centered views that capture the process of leadership and change and that are exemplified in the approach to leadership derived from my study of African American women executives. First is the view that focuses on leadership as the management of meaning. Second is the view that focuses on leadership as socially critical and focused on emancipation and change.

Smircich and Morgan (1982) advanced a view of leadership as the management of meaning. They defined leadership as "... the process whereby one or more individuals succeeds in attempting to frame and define the reality of others" (p. 258). Standing alone, this definition, not surprisingly, leads some to conclude that Smircich and Morgan advocated a monologic view of leadership (see Fairhurst, 2001). However, when viewed within their larger theoretical framework, it is clear that Smircich and Morgan intended a more dialogic, coconstruction focus. Fundamental to their definition is an understanding of leadership as a process of social construction:

> Leadership, like other social phenomena, is socially constructed through interaction (Berger & Luckmann, 1966), emerging as a result of the constructions and actions of both leaders and led. It involves a complicity or process of negotiation through which certain individuals, implicitly or explicitly, surrender their power to define the nature of their experience to others. (Smircich & Morgan, 1982, p. 258)

They further emphasized this negotiated and co-constructed view when they stated "the phenomenon of leadership in being interactive is by nature dialectical. It is shaped through the interaction of at least two points of reference, i.e., of leaders and of led" (pp. 258–259). They added further to this view of leadership as coconstruction in noting the power-based construction of organizational leadership. They asserted "Although leaders draw their power from their [hierarchically legitimated] ability to define the reality of others, their inability to control completely provides the seeds of disorganization in the organization of meaning" (Smircich & Morgan, 1982, p. 259). Thus, from a monologic view, people in formal organizational leadership positions my have the *opportunity* to

LEADERSHIP IN THE POSTINDUSTRIAL ERA

attempt to define and manage the reality of others. Yet a dialogic frame directs attention to the ability and willingness of leaders and followers to recognize the contested context within which that opportunity to manage meaning arises.

Weick's (1978) view of "leader as medium" is very similar to Smircich and Morgan's (1982) approach in emphasizing the negotiated nature of leadership. Focusing on the group level of analysis, Weick argued that leadership is a process of mediating between the group's organizing process (how things should be done) and their informational environment (the varied plausible interpretations of how things should be done, emanating from inside and outside the group). Morgan (1986) also acknowledged the negotiated character of leadership when he argued that leaders do not have to lead by placing themselves in the forefront of action. Instead, he asserted, leaders can play a background role, shaping the stage of action and the general direction that events will take but leaving choice about the details to those responsible for their implementation. However, the desire to implement the leader's directives depends upon whether others see fit to do so.

These views of leadership as the management of meaning conceptualize leadership as a communication accomplishment (Fairhurst, 2001; Garfinkel, 1967). Smircich and Morgan's (1983) definition is especially effective at emphasizing the individual-systems tensions that must be negotiated in everyday leadership situations, for they highlighted the unequal relationship that exists (either explicitly or implicitly) in the leader–follower relationship. However, their definition does not address the notion of change and emancipation.

A critical feminist lens captures the elements of intended social change and emancipation that are crucial in postindustrial views of leadership and that are not emphasized in the Smircich and Morgan definition. More fundamentally, a critical feminist meaning-centered approach to leadership shifts the focus away from structural-functionalist, management-oriented, and traditionally masculine views of leadership and toward the process of leadership and how it can facilitate social change. This positions leadership as a socially critical phenomenon, that is "fundamentally addressed to social change and human emancipation, that it is basically a display of social critique, and that its ultimate goal is the achievement and refinement of human community" (Foster, 1989, p. 46–48). This portrays leadership as a localized, negotiated process of mutual influence that would theoretically accommodate the multiple, often contradictory viewpoints and paradoxical situational challenges of 21st-century organizations (Parker, 2001).

The notion of transformational leadership (Bass, 1985; Bennis & Nanus, 1985; Burns, 1978; Tichy & Devanna, 1986; Rost, 1991) provides a basis for linking the ideas of leadership as the management of meaning and leadership

as a process of social change and emancipation. The notion of transformational leadership was first articulated by Burns (1978) as a process of
evolving interrelationships in which leaders influence followers and are influenced in turn to modify their behavior as they meet responsiveness or resistance. According to Burns (1978), transformational leaders seek to raise the
consciousness of followers by appealing to higher ideals and moral values such
as liberty, justice, equality, peace, and humanitarianism, not to baser emotions
such as fear, greed, jealousy, or hatred. As Yukl (2002) observed, transformational leadership is viewed as both a microlevel influence process between individuals and as a macrolevel process of mobilizing power to change
social systems and reform institutions.

Here, I use Rost's (1991) reinterpretation of Burns (1978) notion of transformation leadership, but with a critical eye toward postindustrial assumptions and
values that Burn's definition does not address. More importantly, Rost's (1991)
definition builds on the strengths of Smircich and Morgan's (1982) definition
(e.g., he implicitly acknowledged the creation of meaning through interaction),
but he placed a critical emphasis on social change through dialogic interaction:

> Leadership is [a multidirectional, noncoercive, but unequal] influence relation-
> ship among leaders and followers [in which the followers are active, and there is
> typically more than one leader in the relationship, and] who intend real changes
> that reflect their mutual purposes. (Rost, 1991, p. 102)

Rost's (1991) definition emphasizes social change and emancipation, as
understood from critical/feminist perspectives. He positioned his work as a critique
of structural functionalism in leadership studies that has been advanced in feminist
scholarship (Buckley & Steffy, 1986; Calàs & Smircich, 1988; Kellerman, 1984),
and emphasized the development of mutual purposes as a way of working toward
emancipation from the oppression of women, ethnic domination, and racial
oppression. Mutual purposes, according to Rost, are "common purposes developed
over time as leaders and followers interact in a noncoercive relationship about the
changes they intend" (p. 151). For leaders and followers steeped in the ambiguous,
corporatized, sexualized and racialized contexts of 21st-century organizations, one
can envision intended changes emerging from such an arrangement might include
progressive activities such as transformation and emancipation from oppressive
and exploitative work processes.

Taken together, Smircich and Morgan (1982) and Rost's (1991) definitions
conceptualize leadership in this way:

> Leadership is an influence relationship among leaders and followers who intend
> real changes that reflect their mutual purposes (Rost, 1991); and these mutual

purposes are negotiated through a process whereby one or more individuals [leaders and followers] succeeds in attempting to frame and define the reality of others (Smircich & Morgan, 1982).

In summary, this view of leadership emphasizes a localized, negotiated process of mutual influence that would theoretically accommodate the multicultural, racialized, often contradictory viewpoints and paradoxical situational challenges of 21st-century organizations (Parker, 2001). I now turn to focus on traditions of African American women's leadership as an exemplar of a meaning centered approach to leadership that focuses on social change and emancipation.

II

African American Women: An Untapped Source of Leadership Knowledge

[I]t is tempting to think that Black women are somehow "naturally" stronger and wiser than the rest of the population, that they are born with more courage and resourcefulness and, perhaps, compassion. But that's no more true that any other stereotype. The values that have helped Black women survive are entirely communicable. And at a time when the problems of our society seem insoluble and the obstacles to peace and freedom insurmountable, all Americans have a great deal to learn from the history of Black women in America.

—Hine & Thompson (1998, p. 308)

This provocative statement was written by historians, Darlene Clark Hine and Kathleen Thompson, at the conclusion of their book on the history of Black women in America, in which they chronicled the lives and achievements of Black women from the seventeenth through twentieth centuries (Hines & Thompson, 1998). Their statement is provocative for two reasons that provide the focus of Part II of this book. First, not only have Black women's achievements not been celebrated throughout history, until recently they have not been acknowledged as important enough to be recorded (Hine & Thompson, 1998). However, as Hine and Thompson noted, in the past two decades, the history of Black women in America has been, and continues to be uncovered, revealing what I would refer to as cultural traditions of survival, resistance, and change. Hine and Thompson corroborated this view when they asserted, "Quite simply, the way Black women approach life works. It cannot overcome

29

all obstacles, but it has enabled Black women to shape the raw materials of their lives into an extraordinary succession of victories, small and large" (p. 5). One goal of Part II is to synthesize and bring to the foreground some traditions of leadership that emerge from African American women's history of survival, resistance and change. Although this is not meant to be a comprehensive historical documentation of the history of Black women in America, I draw upon the work of researchers who make a case for cultural continuity in Black women's history (Giddings, 1984; Hine & Thompson, 1998; Payne, 1995)

The second reason Hine's and Thompson's (1998) claim is provocative is that it emphasizes that cultural traditions are "entirely communicable" across cultures. Although public officials and professionals in organizational settings are becoming increasingly aware of the value of embracing diverse cultural perspectives, not much emphasis has been placed on sharing culturally defined communication competencies and knowledge across gender, racial, socioeconomic, and other cultural boundaries. Rather than simply advancing one cultural tradition as a standard for all others to follow, I argue for a more interactive view of cross-cultural learning that begins with the question: What can we learn from listening closely to the experiences of a particular culture?

Indeed listening represents the most challenging step toward learning from the experiences of African American women. The idea of valuing American women's potential contributions to the production of knowledge may seem counterintuitive in a society in which the devaluation of African American women has been so deeply ingrained (Christian, 1980; Davis, 1981; Lubiano, 1992; Morton, 1991; Walker, 1983). As shown, throughout U.S. history, in popular literature, the news media, television shows, and movies, Black women have been denigrated as *Mammies, Matriarchs, Superwomen, Castrators,* and *Sapphires* (Christian, 1980; Morton, 1991; Walker, 1983), and more recently as *Welfare Queens* and *Over-Achieving Black Ladies* (Lubiano, 1992). In contemporary society, African American women are the victims of these negative stereotypes that dominate the larger culture and even many quarters of Black America (Dyson, 2003). Dyson made the point that acknowledging the contributions of Black women:

> is a crucial way to combat the forces that bring stigma and demonization to [B]lack women's doors.... I think it is undeniable that we live in a society that has failed to acknowledge the full extent of our debt to [B]lack women's gifts. We have often absorbed their wisdom, sucked their lives, appealed to their insight, depended on their strength, desired their beauty, fed on their hope, hungered for their affirmation, sought their approval, and relied on their faith. And yet we have not paid sufficient tribute to how central [B]lack women are to our race, our nation, indeed, our globe, as they have fought for freedom with their hearts, minds,

and souls. Those of us who have benefited from [B]lack women's love ought to
love them back, in the presence of the world. (p. xix)

Similar to Dyson's theme, this book is one effort to counter the discourses
that silence African American women's potential contributions. However,
rather than a general affirmation of Black women's worth, the focus here is on
their specific, rarely acknowledged contributions to the creation of leadership
knowledge. Thus, a second goal of Part II is to illuminate the discourses that devalue African American women and that function to silence African American
women's potential contributions to the production of leadership knowledge.

(EN)COUNTERING DISCOURSES THAT DEVALUE AFRICAN AMERICAN WOMEN

In the following chapters, I discuss historical discourses that have contributed
to an ongoing cultural text that has devalued African American women and
influenced their participation in the workforce from slavery through
21st-century deindustrialization. This cultural text is perpetuated through
derogatory myths and images that are codified through discourses about work
that have shaped, and continue to shape, African American women's work
experiences. I argue that African American women's survival, resistance, and
strategies of change in response to this cultural text reflect a leadership tradition that is useful for re-envisioning leadership in 21st-century organizations.
Focusing on the leadership experiences of some African American women in
United States History, I explore historical accounts of Black pioneer women,
activists, entrepreneurs, and professionals that reveal traditions of African
American women's leadership.

Specifically, my reading of the literature on African American women's labor
force participation reveals two discursive moves that have devalued and
demonized African American women in work contexts and compelled the development of a tradition of leadership: (a) "Black Women as Fallen Woman-
hood/Black Women as 'Natural' Laborers," and (b) "Black Women as Marginal
Workers." These discourses have been influenced in turn by specific economic
conditions that determined Black women's location in systems of power relations, beginning with their forced labor during the era of U.S. enslavement of
Africans, their high poverty rates from the end of slavery into the 1960s, and
their precarious positions in the changing opportunity structures of 20th-cen-
tury urbanization and deindustrialization.

Taking each discourse in historical sequence, in the following chapters I focus on how Black women's resistance to oppressive discourses from the era of

slavery and through the contemporary times reveal a tradition of leadership and organizing that is "entirely communicable" (Hine & Thompson, 1998, p. 308). Chapter 3 takes up the first of these discursive texts and the specific strategies of resistance and leadership African American women enacted in response to these discourses. I argue that it is in the era of slavery that the seeds were planted for the emergence of African American women's tradition of leadership. Then, in chapter 4, I discuss the second discursive text and its corresponding era—Emancipation through the Civil Rights Movement. I argue that it is in this era that a tradition of African American women's leadership begins to take shape as an approach that is applicable to contexts of multicultural change and fragmentation, such as 21st-century organizations.

3

The Seeds of a Tradition of Leadership: Resisting Discourses of "Black Women as Fallen Womanhood/Black Women as 'Natural' Laborers" During U.S.-Institutionalized Slavery

In this chapter I argue that it is in the era of slavery that the seeds were planted for the emergence of African American women's tradition of leadership. Hine and Thompson (1998) made the important point that African women who arrived in the New World during the eighteenth and nineteenth centuries were likely "accustomed to being resourceful, determined, and somewhat independent economically" (p. 11), even in the context of the diverse expressions of patriarchal African cultures from which they were stolen or sold. Therefore, one could argue, as Hine and Thompson did, that the enslaved African woman had the remnants of a cultural advantage that would help her survive in the New World. However, I argue that it is the expression and re-creation of that cultural advantage in the context of U.S. institutionalized slavery—a system that was unique in its brutality, even in a world that regularly sanctioned exploitative labor—that a tradition of African American women's leadership emerged.

Specifically, in this chapter I describe the discursive context in which enslaved African American women were constructed as "fallen womanhood" and as "natural laborers," through derogatory stereotypical images, and how these images influenced particular raced and gendered interactive work contexts. Then, I show how African American women's resistance to these discourses demonstrate a culture of resistance and change that laid the foundation for a tradition of organizing and leadership.

DEROGATORY IMAGES OF AFRICAN AMERICAN WOMEN PRODUCED DURING THE ERA OF SLAVERY

The literature on the sociopolitical history of Black women's labor force participation reveals that during the era of U.S.-institutionalized slavery, images of White women as idealized womanhood and Black women as devalued or fallen womanhood codified certain discourses about Black women and work (Burgess & Horton, 1993; Harley, 1997; Jones, 1985; White, 1985). These images were discursively (re)produced within a context of racist assumptions about womanhood, in which the idealized attributes of "true womanhood" are assigned to White women, whereas Black women are cast as fallen womanhood (Christian, 1980; Morton, 1991; Welter, 1966). The elevated status of an ideal White womanhood throughout history has been crucially reinforced by this racial representation of *Bad Womanhood*. These images continue even today to influence perceptions about African American women in society in general and in the workplace in particular (Bell & Nkomo, 2001).

Stereotypes of Black Women as "Bad Womanhood"

The representation of Bad Black Womanhood took shape during the era of slavery as stereotypes that ultimately labeled Black women as: *Sapphire*, the sexualized, cunning, deceitful, and bad tempered servant; *Mammy*, the inept and comical domestic servant; and *the Matriarch*, the masculinized, domineering, version of Mammy (King, 1973; Morton, 1991). As Morton observed, "together these images shaped the composite picture of a defeminized female failure" (p. 7). Moreover, they served as a basis for White slaveholders to take a crudely opportunistic approach toward the labor of enslaved women.

One predominant image of African American women as fallen womanhood was created in part by the racist sexual stereotypes of Black women during the era of slavery as cunning and deceitful, and with bad tempers and loose sexual morals (Fra-Molinero, 1995; Morton, 1991). Sometimes referred to as the *Jezzabel stereotype* (White, 1985), and embodied as Sapphire in the 1950s sitcom

Amos and Andy, an image of Black women as "sassy and sexualized" was developed in the stereotypical figure of the *negra* in popular theater dating back to 16th- and 17th-century Spain (Fra-Molinero, 1995). Old World historical texts and Spanish literary representations of Black enslaved women produced stereotypes of Black women as a threat to White families that were eventually exported to the New World. These stereotypes functioned to create and justify Black women's marginality, exploitation, and control in a way that was unique to a plantation economy (Fra-Molinero, 1995; Vaz, 1995). Morton (1991) described the context of this stereotype as one in which there was "a double standard that prescribed female purity, and yet ignored White men's sexual exploitation of Black women[;]the plantation mistress blamed the enslaved woman, not the slaveholder, for miscegenation" (p. 9). At the same time, the dehumanization of enslaved Black women—for example being forced to disrobe for inspection at slave auctions—served as a basis for the White slaveholder to rationalize his violation of black female sexual purity as no violation at all (Clinton, 1982), and, as discussed later, to justify exploiting the productive and reproductive labor of enslaved women in a culture that purportedly elevated the status of women (Harley, 1997).

Another stereotype, the Mammy, is perhaps the most prominent one that emerged out of the era of U.S.-institutionalized slavery (Christian, 1980. It is an image that emerges from Southern life and literature that is remarkable in the way that it has been created and recreated throughout history. For example, one Mammy stereotype paradoxically symbolized the ideal slave and the ideal woman. As portrayed in films, such as *Gone With the Wind,* the Mammy figure is portrayed as a maternal figure who loved the White children whom she nursed and raised, while she was in charge of all domestic management, in effect as the "surrogate mistress and mother" (Morton, 1991, p. 10; White, 1985). However, "in reality, no one [enslaved] woman served all these roles" (White, 1985, p. 49).

Christian's (1980) reading of Old South literature revealed the Mammy stereotype as a racial and sexual subtext that functioned to make credible the idealized image of the *White Lady.* "[T]he ... Mammy was invariably cast as superreligious and loyal to 'her' [W]hite family, and also as physically strong, tough, obese, and ugly. Her masculinization highlighted the Lady's ultra-femininity" (p. 12). This characterization of Black women as the masculinized opposite of White women reinforced another enduring myth about Black womanhood, that of the Black Matriarch.

The myth of the Black Matriarch in some ways represents a composite of the images of Bad Black Womanhood that emerged during the era of slavery and that have been perpetuated throughout history. White (1985) argued that the contemporary image of African American women as "a domineering Black woman who consumes men circles back to the Jezebel [/Sapphire] slave-seductress figure, while 'her assertive demeanor identifies her with Mammy'" (p. 166).

Constructing Black Women as "Natural" Laborers

As they were reinforced in popular literature and social contexts, racist and sexist images about Black womanhood made it socially acceptable to view Black women as exploitable laborers, doing work that fit the traditional roles of both White women and Black men (Burgess & Horton, 1993; Jones, 1985). As Jones (1985) pointed out, in the context of the sexual division of labor in the U.S. plantation economy, the work of Black men and White women conformed to patterns similar to those in other parts of the country:

> Despite the rhetorical glorification of the slaveholder's wife as the embodiment of other worldly virtues, she remained responsible for conventional womanly duties in the mundane realm of household management. Likewise, slave men performed duties [such as planting, weeding, harvesting crops, clearing pasture, and mending fences] similar to those of New England and southern yeomen farmers. (p. 12)

However, for Black enslaved women, racial and patriarchal ideologies intersected to facilitate the pursuit of profit, so that the traditional sexual division of labor did not apply to them (Jones, 1995). The racial ideology of Black women as Bad Women allowed for their exploitation as laborers alongside men in the production of staple crops. A slaveholder just as 'naturally' put his bondswomen to work chopping cotton as washing, ironing, or cooking, and performing "a reproductive function vital to individual slaveholder's financial interests and to the inherently expansive system of slavery in general" (Jones, 1995, p. 12). Patriarchal and capitalist assumptions concerning women's work (e.g., the control of women's bodies) facilitated the exploitation of enslaved Black women as serving a reproductive function.

Black Women's Strategies For Survival, Resistance, and Change During The Era of Slavery[1]

Several strategies for survival, resistance, and change were borne out of Black women's struggle to combat the oppression of slavery and the controlling images that reified a racialized and sexualized cultural text (Aptheker, 1982; Collins, 1990, 1998a; Hine & Thomson, 1998; Jones, 1985; Morton, 1991). Indeed, Collins (1990) argued persuasively that it is the process of negotiating and reconciling identities that has historically informed African American women's strategies for empowerment, both through individual agency and collective action (Collins, 1990, 1998a; hooks, 1981; Jones, 1985). Significantly, many of these strategies emerged from enslaved Black women and men's attempts to sustain their family life in the face of the callousness of slaveholders, mistresses, and overseers (Jones, 1985). These resistance strategies have continued to influence African American life for generations and are consistent themes in Black feminist writings about empowerment (cf., Collins, 1990; Cooper, 1892; Gilkes, 1980; Hine & Thompson, 1998; hooks, 1981; Hull, Scott, & Smith., 1982; King, 1988; Lorde, 1984; Rogers-Rose, 1980; Springer, 1999).

Specifically, five themes related to African American women's resistance and empowerment are revealed in the literature on Black women's struggle to combat the oppression of slavery: (1) being self defined, (2) being self determined, (3) developing and using voice, (4) connecting to and building community, and (5) seeking spirituality and regeneration.

Being Self-Defined. One theme that corresponds to Black women's strategies for survival, resistance, and change during the era of slavery is being self-defined. Collins (1990, 1998a) described a Black feminist standpoint perspective that conceptualizes *self-definition* as the power to name one's own reality. Often, in defiance of the slaveholders' tendencies to ignore gender differences in making assignments in the fields, enslaved Black women, whenever possible adhered to a more strict division of labor within their own households and communities (Jones, 1985). However, to ensure the survival of the family even as family members were sold away, family roles were kept flexible. "Adults of whatever relationship took over the parenting responsibilities for children when necessary. Brothers and sisters provided care and support for each other" (Hine & Thompson, 1998, p. 20). Thus a fundamental resistance strategy, borne out of the degradation of Black women during slavery, is to define in ones own terms what a woman or a man ought to do. It is a strategy that rejects the very notion that gender roles can be viewed as fixed.

Being Self-Determined. Related to the theme of self-definition is self-determination, the power to decide one's own destiny (Collins, 1998a). Black women during the slave era were important influences in promoting Black self-determination as a form of resistance to the institution of slavery. Freed women of the North, such as Maria Stewart, Mary Ann Shadd Cary, Sarah Parker Remond, Sojourner Truth, and the legendary Harriet Tubman, were active in their efforts to promote Black self-determination, especially for Black women. Both Stewart and Cary were published authors and, like Remond and Truth gave public addresses speaking out against slavery and seeking to draw attention to Black women's concerns. Maria Stewart is noted as the first American woman to lecture publicly to an audience of both Black and White women and men. Her message, such as her lecture in Boston in 1832, was often centered on the abolition of slavery, but she also emphasized self-determination and economic independence for African Americans. Stewart "demanded that Black women take an active part in business, politics, and education, and that they uphold the highest moral standards, in order to refute the myths of the [W]hite South that said [B]lack women were ignorant, lazy, and degenerate" (Hine & Thompson, 1998, p. 107).

The legendary Harriet Ross Tubman, who has achieved "fame of mythic proportions as the best-known conductor on the Underground Railroad" (p. 115), is perhaps the most widely acknowledged example of Black women's self determination (Hine & Thompson, 1998). The *railroad* was a network of "stops" along several routes, going from the South to the North to Canada, the sole purpose being to help enslaved people escape from the South. The *station masters* were White and Black men and women who "risked their lives to offer refuge, usually in their homes, to those who were running desperately to freedom" (p. 115). After making her own escape to freedom in 1849, Tubman returned to make as many as 11 to 15 trips into the South to rescue more than 200 people and deliver them to freedom (Hine & Thompson, 1998).

Developing and Using Voice.   Developing and using *voice* is a third theme related to Black women's strategies for survival, resistance, and change during the era of slavery. Voice through the uses of agency and activism is a conceptualization of resistance and empowerment employed in Black feminist writing as early as the nineteenth century (Cooper, 1892), and more recently in the writings of hooks (1990), Collins (1998a), and others (see Springer, 1999). During the era of slavery, Black women's voice as agency and activism is revealed in extraordinary achievements that were remarkable, given the oppressive conditions that served as a social context. As shown in the recently recovered histories of Black women in America, a Black woman's achievements of this era varied sometimes, but not always, in accordance with whether she was free or enslaved or whether she was enslaved in the South or in the North (Hine & Thompson, 1998; Lerner, 1972; Vaz, 1995).

Hine and Thompson (1998) highlighted the lives of formerly enslaved women (or those born into freed families) in the North, such as Phillis Wheatley, Elizabeth Freeman, Lucy Terry Prince of Massachusetts, and Elleanor Eldridge of Rhode Island, each of whom managed to influence their

THE SEEDS OF TRADITION OF LEADERSHIP

communities through their, resourcefulness, entrepreneurship, and oratory. For example, Phillis Wheatley is now well known as America's first Black published author, publishing a book of poems in 1773 (Hine, 1993). Less well known are Elizabeth Freeman, who "sued for her freedom in 1781 and won, basing her case on the new constitution of Massachusetts" and Elleanor Eldridge who "owned a wallpaper business and sold the best cheese in the town of Warwick, Rhode Island (Hine & Thompson, 1998, p. 4). Lucy Terry Prince stood before the trustees of Williams College in Massachusetts and gave an "earnest and eloquent speech of three hours, quoting an abundance of law and Gospel," in her attempt to gain admission of one of her sons, who was ultimately denied because of his race. (Sheldon, quoted in Hine & Thompson, pp. 2–3). Later, remarkably, she argued and won a case before the United States Supreme Court in which "A Colonel Eli Bronson tried to steal a lot belonging to the Princes in Sunderland, near the home of Ethan Allen (Hine & Thompson, 1998, p. 3).

Indeed, Lucy Terry Prince's oratory is indicative of what Logan (1999) proclaims as nineteenth century African American women's full participation "in the verbal warfare for human dignity" (p. 1). Logan's comprehensive treatise on the persuasive discourse of 19th-century Black women reveals that,

African American women addressed women's organizations, church groups, antislavery associations, and temperance unions. They spoke in all sections of the United States, in Canada, and in the British Isles. They spoke to [B]lack audiences, [W]hite audiences, and mixed audiences on the panoply of issues challenging peoples of African descent throughout America at the time. In addition to the oppressive defining issue of slavery, these concerns included employment, civil rights, women's rights, emigration, and self-improvement. After the Civil War, mob violence, racial uplift, and support for the Southern [B]lack woman were added to the list. (pp. 1–2)

Not surprisingly, voice as a resistance strategy took a very different form in the lives of enslaved Black women in the South than that of free Black women in the North. As Hine and Thomson (1998) noted, had Prince, Freeman, or Eldridge been brought to this country and sold to a southern plantation owner in 1800, they would have occupied a status "little higher than livestock" (p. 3). Direct resistance in the enslaved population was often met with terrible punishment from White slaveholders and overseers. Therefore, the more usual course was to find a covert way of resisting the conditions of slavery, and this sometimes took on the character of negotiation.

In law, the power of the slaveholder was absolute. In practice, many factors entered into the relationship between owner and slave. Personalities were significant, as well as strength of character. The desire on the part of the slaveholding family to live a peaceful, pleasant life was often of great consequence in the negotiation. Women who lived and worked in the Big House were able to take advantage of these factors to chip away at the power of the owners. This was one of that there were different styles of resistance for women and for men. Women were more likely to engage in verbal and even physical confrontations, while men far more often ran away. (p. 93)

In the context of the southern plantation, Black enslaved women's achievements were the everyday resistances to the oppressive conditions of slavery—negotiating an "acceptable level of work, shelter, food, punishment, and free time" (White, 1985, quoted in Hine & Thompson, 1998, p. 91). An enslaved Black woman might have used sabotage in her effort to earn the right to change job sites, or using a more direct tactic, refuse to work, being supported by other women in the community in her protest (Hine & Thompson, 1998). In a remarkable example of initiative, negotiation, and market savvy, enslaved Black women of mid-1600 Charles Town (later Charleston, South Carolina), wrestled control of the town market through selling, buying, and reselling goods. Drawing on their skills as former West African traders, the women negotiated with their slaveholders to take the money from selling plantation goods to buy other goods and resell them, making a larger profit, and paying the slaveholder a stable wage, and keeping the rest of the profits for herself. Through this practice, frequently challenged (to no avail) by laws and procedures to stop it, some of the women amassed considerable wealth (Hine & Thompson, 1998).

The experiences of both freed and enslaved women affirm that African American women's achievements "did not grow out of degradation but out of a legacy of courage, resourcefulness, initiative, and dignity that goes back to 1619" (Hine & Thompson, 1998, p. 4).

Connecting to and Building Community

Another theme in the literature on Black women's struggle to combat the oppression of slavery and the controlling images of Black womanhood is connecting to and building community. Indeed beginning in the era of slavery in the United States, African American women have demonstrated a long history of activism through community work (Gilkes, 1980; McCluskey, 1997). Activism through community work consists of activities to strengthen family and kinship ties, combat racism, and empower communities to survive, grow, and advance, thus reinforcing the theme, *lifting as we climb* (Gilkes, 1980; McCluskey, 1997).

Jones (1985) documented the role of the Black family in strengthening and building connections among the community of enslaved people. She noted that, Slave family life, as the cornerstone of Afro-American culture, combined an African heritage with American exigencies, and within the network of kin relationships Black women and men sought to express their respect for each other even as they resisted the intrusiveness of Whites (p. 43).

Leadership in the community of enslaved people was expressed through informal, everyday means, with the most important roles in the community reserved for those who performed services for other enslaved people rather than for Whites (Blassingame, 1979). Black women played important leadership roles in the community of enslaved people as they worked to help to preserve the community through education, healthcare, spiritual leadership, and support for the slavery resistance movement.

African American women were primary in providing education to children and adults in the enslaved communities. Education, specifically learning to read and write, was considered a tool for emancipation, a means of liberation (Quint, 1970). However, beginning in the mid-1700s, formal education was illegal for enslaved people, and teachers risked severe punishment to educate their family members and others in the community. The teachers either learned to read or write on their own, or were taught by wives of White slaveholders, religious groups, freed African Americans, and abolitionists (Gyant, 1990). Classes were often held late at night in the slave church, in someone's home, or outside, miles from the plantation. Materials used were the Bible, books taken from the plantation, and newspapers (Gyant). For example, Milla Granson, a woman born into slavery in Kentucky around 1800, and eventually sold to a plantation owner in Mississippi, educated hundreds of African American children and adults (Hine, 1993). Taught to read by her former slaveholder's children, Granson taught other enslaved people to read and write, many of eventually wrote their own passes to freedom. In Mississippi, Granson conducted a school in a small cabin that ran from midnight to 2:00 a.m. each day, graduating more than 200 students. Her efforts eventually led to the implementation of a Mississippi law that made it legal for enslaved people to teach each other (Hine, 1993).

In addition to education, enslaved women's work for other community members included healthcare, spirituality, and support of the resistance movement. Elderly women were especially revered for their knowledge of the healing arts, and their service as midwife, healer, and spiritual leaders. More generally, African American women served their communities by challenging the slaveholder's authority in direct ways. For example, "as the persons in charge of food preparation for both [W]hites and their own families, women at times clandestinely fed runaways in an effort to keep them out of harm's way for as long as possible" (Jones, 1985, p. 43).

Thus when it emerged from bondage, the "[B]lack family had a highly developed sense of itself as an institution protective of the community at large" (p. 43).

Seeking Spirituality and Regeneration. A final theme suggests that African American women's empowerment through resistance is most effective when it is sustained through energies that elevate the human spirit and create new strategies for liberation from oppressive situations (Collins, 1998a; Omalade, 1994). *Spirituality and regeneration* can be defined as a reliance on a spiritual center for answers, explanations, and focus toward the future. It is a counternarrative to the seemingly tragic, singular images of Black women's strength: the "long suffering mother ('Life for me ain't been no crystal stair') and the indomitable grandmother, pillar of strength and wisdom to all who know her" (Jones, 1985, p. 9). A more complex understanding of strength demonstrated in the lives of African American women throughout history must take into account the role of spirit and spiritual life as a source of healing, joy, and empowerment, and liberation. As Collins (1998a) asserted, spirituality continues to move countless African American women to struggle in everyday life. Similarly, Omalade (1994) argued that African American women's empowerment "cannot be understood without knowing her spirit and spiritual life" (cited in Collins, 1998a, p. 247).

In their seminal book and documentary film series, *This Far By Faith: Stories from the African American Religious Experience*, Williams and Dixie (2003), traced the story of how religious faith has inspired the African American struggle for freedom from slavery through the Civil Rights movement that continues today. Stripped of their native religious traditions, along with their names and sometimes family, "Black people used the [slaveholders'] religion to defeat slavery ... [by taking] on a cloak of faith, an unshakable belief that God would carry them through slavery and lift them up to freedom" (p. 2).

Although history most often documents the courageous acts and achievements of Black male religious leaders, there is evidence that Black women's faith-inspired resistance, beginning in the era of slavery, was an invaluable resource in the struggle for freedom. The most noted is Sojourner Truth, whose absolute faith transformed her into a champion in the fight to end slavery. Harriet Tubman and others' appropriation of spiritual hymns as a secret code for those bound for the Underground Railroad is another well-known example. Other women, such as Sarah Allen, wife of Richard Allen,[2] were in the shadows of their more noted husbands, but they, too, along with countless other African American women understood the power of faith in resisting oppression. Katy Ferguson, born into slavery but gaining her freedom by the age of 18, used what her mother had taught her about Christian scripture to start a Sunday school for

Black and White children who lived in the poor New York City neighborhood in which she lived in 1793. The school later gained support and recognition as the Murray Street Sabbath School, New York's first Sunday School (Hine & Thompson, 1998).

 The resistance themes borne out of the struggle to combat the oppression of slavery formed the foundation for African American women's survival and resistance in the racial and patriarchal systems of domination that persisted after the end of U.S. institutionalized slavery, through reconstruction, the Great Depression, WWII and the Civil Rights Movement of the 1950s and 1960s. It is during these 100 turbulent years that a tradition of African American women's leadership based on resistance, organizing, and transformation is visible.

ENDNOTES

1. In her incisive analysis of resistance and struggle in the history of Black women's work since slavery, Jones (1985) made the important point that "forces that conspired to keep [B]lack women and men in their inferior place also helped to undermine the economic security of non-elite [W]hites as well" (p. 8). Her call for analyses of the interrelationships among work, sex, and class to explore the plight of, for example, wives of White sharecroppers ... Eastern European immigrant women working in factories, bears repeating.
2. In 1816, Richard Allen founded the African Methodist Episcopal Church, the oldest historically African American religious denomination, which grew out of Bethel Church established in Philadelphia in 1794.

4

Forging a Tradition of Leadership: Resisting Discourses of "Black Women as Marginal Workers" From Legal Emancipation Through the Civil Rights Movement

Within the context of sweeping social, cultural, and economic changes that occurred in the 100 years after the end of U.S.-institutionalized slavery, the five themes of resistance and activism that emerged from African American women's struggle during the era of slavery are even more visible as a tradition of leadership. In this chapter I show how during this era, African American women in rural and urban areas of the North and South were constructed as a particular kind of marginal worker at the intersection of race and gender-based systems of domination. Additionally, I discuss how this marginalization existed for both the majority of African American women in working-class jobs and for the small but growing number of Black women that had entered and were continuing to enter the professions. The chapter concludes with a discussion of how African American women's resistance to the cultural text of marginalization infused a tradition of leadership that crystallized during the Civil Rights Movement of the 1960s.

DISCOURSES OF "BLACK WOMEN
AS MARGINAL WORKERS"

From the end of U.S. institutionalized slavery through the 1960s, a second discursive text took shape that reinforced the images of African American
women as a certain kind of devalued and marginalized worker. In the racist
and patriarchal systems of post Civil War America, African American women
were forced to work in "only those jobs considered unfit for White men, White
women, and Black men" (Aptheker, 1982, p. 137). This trend continued
through the end of World War II, as the majority of African America women in
both urban and rural areas of the North, South, and West were forced into agricultural, domestic, or laundry work, or allied fields (Aptheker). This
marginalization also held true for African American women entrepreneurs
and those working in middle-class professions.

The End of Slavery Through Reconstruction

As the institution of slavery gradually disintegrated during and after the Civil
War, formerly enslaved African Americans began the process of attempting to
control their own labor and family life (Jones, 1985). Many of them traveled from
town to town looking for their children, mothers, wives, husbands, or other relatives that had been sold to other plantation owners in previous years. Even as they
were attempting to rebuild and provide for their families, they were confronted
with the decision to remain linked to southern plantations or to travel to nearby
towns or to the North or West to search for work. Most remained in the South
and worked for wages as field hands and domestic servants for former slaveholders. African American women with children, many of them widowed, were forced
to take whatever work was available to help sustain their families, and that usually
meant remaining linked to White plantation owners (Jones, 1985). Depending
on White employers for payment was often a problem. According to grievances
filed by African American women under the Freedman's Bureau, "many workers
were routinely—and ruthlessly—defrauded of the small amounts they had
earned and then 'run off the place'" (p. 54).
   In the late 1860s the sharecropping system was established that promised to provide some sense of autonomy and stability but that preserved a stagnant postbellum
economy that eventually ensnared poor Whites as well as freedmen and women
(Jones, 1985, p. 61). Under the 50–50 sharecropping system, African American
families lived in small houses scattered about the plantation, farmed the small plots
of land parceled out to them, and returned one half of the crop in exchange for ra-
tions and supplies from the planters. However the unscrupulous linking of personal

financial credit to crop liens, and debt penalties enforced by criminal statutes, the system quickly evolved into an exploitative one not very different from slavery that lasted into the twentieth century (Hine & Thompson, 1998; Jones, 1985)

African American women heads of households were often the most exploited in this system (Hine & Thompson, 1998; Jones, 1985). The federally funded Freedman's Bureau set up to support freed families, legitimated a traditional role of the African American husband as the head of his family, and used this to set up unequal compensation for freed men and women and their families. Federal guidelines mandated that African American women receive less compensation than male heads of households. Moreover, federal agents often gave out less land to families with female household heads than for their male counterparts (Jones, 1985).

For married African American women the sharecropping arrangement usually meant having primary responsibility for domestic duties in the home and working along side their husband and children when their labor was needed. African American women's (and their husband's) desire for them to forgo the degradation of field work was met with disdain by southern landowners who saw it as "acting the lady," when, in the eyes of White southerners, "no Black women could actually be a lady" (Hine & Thompson, p. 153). By insisting that women and children could not live in the house that was provided if they did not work, landowners would often try to force women and children into the fields so that more work would be done and a larger crop raised (Hine & Thompson, 1998).

Even as work shifted to more industrialized labor, African American women workers were totally excluded from even the most menial factory labor (the site of relatively higher wages) until the end of the First World War, with the exception of the Southern crab, tobacco, and textile factories where they continued doing the unskilled seasonal work they had done since slavery (Aptheker, 1982). In both rural and urban African American women found work as best they could, often adjusting their employment according to their families needs (Jones, 1985). In rural areas, Black women helped to manage sharecrop land or they labored as wage workers in cotton or tobacco fields, and in the sugar plantations of Louisiana. In the emerging African American urban neighborhoods of the South during this time, African American women did mostly wage work, predominantly as domestics or laundresses, but also as seasonal workers on nearby farms. A few went into to town to sell goods, such as vegetables, chickens, and eggs.

Jim Crow, Industrialization, and the Great Migration North

The oppressive Jim Crow system that began in the 1860s and persisted through the 1950s worked against the hopes of economic opportunity for African Americans in the South. The era of Jim Crow in the southern United States is de-scribed as "a determined and largely successful effort on the part of [W]hite southerners to rob African Americans of all political power, economic opportu-nity, and social equality" (Hine & Thompson, 1998, p. 167). State sanctioned violence, terrorism, and segregation were used in attempts to deny African Americans the right to vote, own land, or to have equal access to public venues such as schools restaurants, parks, libraries, bathrooms, and railway cars.

From about 1900 to 1920, more than 2 million African Americans migrated to the northern industrialized cities (Henri, 1975). However, African American workers were disadvantaged relative to the mostly European immigrant workers preferred by industrial employers (Jones, 1985). African American women were limited to jobs that reinforced a connection to domestic and agricultural work—mechanized steam laundries, meat slaughtering and packing houses, and crab and peanut factories (Aptheker, 1982). In addition to those who were marginalized in U.S. factories of the 1920s, the vast majority of African Ameri-can women worked in what many considered the equally demeaning domain of domestic work (Dill, 1979; Jones, 1985). By 1930, 60% of all African American women employed were in domestic work (Aptheker, 1982).

Depression Era Through Post-World War II

During the Depression era, African American women continued to be marginalized into jobs subordinate to their White female and Black male coun-terparts. In the South, they were generally excluded from relatively stable jobs provided by the New Deal public works programs, such as the Works Progress Administration (WPA). "[Plantation owners [and] government officials ... saw [B]lack wives and mothers chiefly as domestic servants or manual laborers, out-side the pale of the ([W]hite) sexual division of labor" (Jones, 1985, p. 220). For example, WPA officials often served as de facto recruiting agents for local plant-ers. In Oklahoma, a WPA official closed a Black women's work project upon the appearance of "an abundant cotton crop which is in full picking flower" (p.220).

African American women in the North tended to fare a little better than their counterparts in the South during the Depression era. However, they too were seen as expendable members of the labor force. African American women were often the first to be laid off when government policies caused industrial employers to reduce the number of their workers (Jones, 1985).

During World War II, certain men's jobs in factories were redesignated as women's work, and downgraded to a lower pay and status, but other jobs "were converted to Black women's work of even greater inferiority. In airplane assembly plants, [B]lack women stood in stifling 'dope rooms' filled with nauseating fumes of glue, while White women sat on stools in the well-ventilated sewing room" (Jones, 1985, p. 240). After the war, Both White and Black women quickly lost their jobs (some went to returning soldiers, others were simply eliminated). Black women factory workers were "demobilized and redomesticated" (p. 256).

Middle-Class Black Women's Work From Reconstruction Through World War II

Throughout the history of Black people in America, communities of the African American elite existed in northern, eastern, southern, and western cities that comprised people in the professions and an entrepreneurial class. The growth of these communities gained momentum during the years following the Civil War (Jones, 1985; Hine & Thompson, 1998). Although the late-nineteenth and early-twentieth century was a time when African American women were slowly making strides into the professions—mostly in education, but also in medicine, law, pharmacy, the military, aviation, the arts, media, and business and commerce—they continued to be subordinated compared to their White male and female and Black male contemporaries.[1] For example, from the late 1850s through 1900, Black women struggled to gain entry into sex-segregated medical schools for White women, although they had greater success in gaining entry to the Black male dominated medical schools, such as those at Howard University and Meharry Medical College in Nashville, Tennessee. In 1864, Rebecca Lee became the first Black woman doctor in the United States, the one and only Black woman to earn a degree from The New England Female Medical College in Boston. By 1900, a little more than 60 women had earned medical degrees, mostly from Howard and Meharry (Aptheker, 1982).

African American women in affluent communities exhibited a dual focus on achievement and working for social justice. Indeed, as shown in the next section, one of the most important Black resistance movements—the Black Women's Club Movement—emerged from communities of the African American elite, particularly Boston, New York, and Washington, D.C., and it is exemplary of a tradition of African American women's leadership that is grounded in a culture of resistance that crosses class statuses (Collins, 1998a; Jones, 1985).

BLACK WOMEN'S STRATEGIES FOR SURVIVAL, RESISTANCE, AND CHANGE FROM RECONSTRUCTION THROUGH THE CIVIL RIGHTS MOVEMENT

The five themes of resistance and activism that emerged from Black women's struggle during the era of slavery are visible during the eras of reconstruction and the Depression and through the 1960s. These themes became even more visible as a tradition of African American women's leadership based on resistance, organizing, and transformation.

Reconstruction and Into The Twentieth Century: Resistance Through Community Building

The ambiguity, uncertainty, and intense racial hatred African Americans faced in the Jim Crow era—the period just after slavery ended—gave rise to a Black civil society that provided a safe haven but also inspired the development of Black female-run organizations of the Black Women's Club Movement, and courageous and outspoken Black feminist leaders. Comprised of families, churches, social clubs, fraternal organizations, and other organizations, the Black civil society was "a set of institutions, communication networks, and practices that facilitated responses to economic and political challenges confronting Black people" (Collins, 1998a, p. 23). For Black women, one response was in the form of Black women-led organizations devoted to the survival and prosperity of the Black community.

Perhaps the most noted of these clubs emerged out of communities of the Black elite in Boston, New York, and Washington, DC. They were formed by "the daughters, and granddaughters of families that had been free for generations, building modest fortunes; ... the wives of respectable Black working men—barbers, porters, postal workers; ... and the dressmakers and hairdresser who made up such a significant portion of the Black entrepreneurial class" (Hine & Thompson, 1998, p. 178). In 1895, the National Association of Colored Women (NACW) merged two national organizations of Black women's clubs—15 years before the formation of the National Association for the Advancement of Colored People (NAACP), one of the nation's largest civil rights organizations. The motto of the NACW, "lifting as we climb," emphasized the organization's commitment to community and its roots in a culture of resistance that began in the era of U.S. institutionalized slavery (Collins, 1990, 1998a).

Indeed, the genius of the women's vision of organizing the Black women's clubs is in their focus on community building at the local level and connecting this to the larger mission of social justice and human rights. Black women across the country formed thousands of organizations to promote the welfare of their communities, fighting the widespread poverty, illiteracy, and discrimination that abounded during the period of reconstruction and beyond (Jones, 1985). Many African American clubwomen organized schools to educate the millions of African American children and freed adults that lived in the South after the Civil War, and to train teachers to work in African American schools (Hine,

1993, p. 385). For example, in 1886, Lucy Laney founded the Haines Normal and Industrial Institute in Augusta, Georgia. Mary McLeod Bethune taught at the Haines School, and then in 1904, established the Daytona Normal and Industrial School for Negro Girls, which later became Bethune-Cookman College. Nannie Burroughs was founder (1909) and longtime president of the National Training School for Women and Girls in Washington, D.C.

In addition to organizing schools, individual African American women played a crucial role in the massive task of educating African Americans after the end of slavery. They worked as teachers in schools created by large federal and private organizations, such as the Freedman's Bureau, the American Missionary Association, and The Friends Freedman's Association, creating progressive curricula that emphasized both vocational training and education in the liberal arts (Hine, 1993).

The Black church was often the site for the formation of many Black women's clubs, emerging from both a desire to advance community empowerment efforts and a concern for Black women's rights within the entrenched patriarchy of the Black church. Nannie Burrough's outspoken eloquence at the National Baptist Convention (NBC) in 1900 "articulated the righteous discontent of women in the Black Baptist church and served as a catalyst for the formation of the Woman's Convention Auxiliary to the NBC [the largest Black women's organization in America]" (Hine, 1993, p. 201). Eventually, many African American women had leadership roles in the newly formed civil rights organizations, such as the National Association for the Advancement of Colored People (NAACP) and the National Urban League, that were largely dominated by African American male preachers and community leaders.

Additionally, it was through their community work in late-19th and early-20th century Black civil society that individual African American women's leadership as *race women* in the Black Women's Club Movement became visible (Collins, 1998a; Horne, 2000; Jones, 1985). In the context of the times, "African Americans infused the term *race* with a ... meaning signifying cultural identity and heritage" (Collins, 1998a, p. 23; also see Horne, 2000) in contrast to the pseudoscientific notions of race as meaning inferiority and superiority. In addition to the thousands of race women in the Black Women's Club Movement are several who are among the most historically noted. These include Anna Julia Cooper, Ida Gibbs, Mary Jane Patterson, Mary Church Terrell, and Fanny Jackson Coppin, the first Black women to complete a 4-year course of study from an accredited American college (Oberlin College; Hine, 1993). Also noted are Ida B. Wells, who is renown for organizing a national anti-lynching campaign, and Mary McLeod Bethune, as already mentioned, founder of Bethune-Cookman College in 1904, but also founding president of the National Council of Negro Women, advisor and close associate and advisor to Eleanor and President Franklin D. Roosevelt, and arguably "one of the most important Black Americans in history" (Hine, 1993, p.126).

Through their writing, speaking, and organizing, these women and others were vital forces in their work to address the issues important to the national Black community and in the fight for women's rights. Even as they gained international notoriety in their work, they remained closely tied to and integrated in the larger network of the Black Women's Club movement.

Other individual women established themselves as entrepreneurs, but maintained a dual focus on achievement and working for social justice and change. Two noted women pioneers of the West, Bridget (Biddy) Mason and Mary Pleasants, exemplify the entrepreneurial spirit of the era. Both born during the era of slavery, these self-determined and resourceful women amassed great wealth, working to organize for social justice and change in California. Biddy Mason, according to historical accounts, walked to San Bernardino, California from Hancock County, Mississippi and won her freedom in the California courts. Working as a confinement nurse at the rate of $2.50 per day she saved her money and amassed her fortune by buying property in Los Angeles. However, her life's work was working for social justice for people of all races. She spent her time and money visiting and feeding prisoners in jail and organizing efforts to help the homeless and less fortunate (Davis, 1982). She was a founding member of the First African Methodist Episcopal Church (AMEC) in Los Angeles, and established a nursery and day-care center for the children of Black working parents (Hine, 1993).

Mary Ellen Pleasants is noted as demonstrating financial genius during the Gold Rush era in San Francisco. Although historical accounts of her place of birth are conflicting (some accounts report she was born into slavery in the south, Pleasants said she was born in Philadelphia), it is clear that she amassed a fortune in San Francisco during the Gold Rush era, speculating in the stock market, and operating a string of elegant restaurants and "ultra-fashionable boarding houses" (Davis, 1982). At the same time, she was a key figure in the abolitionist movement and the fight for women's rights.

Common strategies in Black women's organizing and leadership after slavery and into the twentieth century were those that emphasized self-definition, self-determination, spirituality, and speaking out against racism, sexism, and other social injustices. For example, local Black women's clubs included mottos and names, such as "Do What You Can," as a reminder to engage in activities that were "always in opposition to the [oppression of the White power structure]" (Jones, 1985, p. 146). The women's work in these clubs and in education included grassroots strategies and tactics—such as empowering people through direct contact and developing inclusive organizing practices—that reappeared in the work of women in the Civil Rights Movement of the 1960s (Payne, 1995), and in the leadership practices of some of the African American women who were the first to enter into the professions.

Depression Era Through the Postwar Years: Resistance and Transformation at Work

Urbanization and industrialization of the early-twentieth century was a back-drop for African American women's leadership in union organizing and other forms of worker resistance strategies. Although the early labor movement touched only a fraction all Black women workers, Harley (1997) documented Black women's efforts to organize unions and other union-like organizations, despite the "race- and gender-exclusionary policies of most early twenti-eth-century labor unions and Black women's large presence in traditionally 'unorganizable' agricultural and domestic jobs" (p. 46). For example, in the late-19th century, Victoria Earle Matthews organized the White Rose Indus-trial Association formed "to protect Black female domestic workers, especially recent migrants from the South, from being either exploited by employment bureaus or forced into prostitution" (Terberg-Penn, 1985, cited in Harley, 1997). In a similar vein, in 1920 Nannie Burroughs organized the National Association of Women Wage Earners as part of a multifaceted strategy to im-prove the lives of Black women wage earners in Washington D.C., especially domestic workers (Harley, 1997, p. 45).

However, it was in the day-to-day context of the shop floor where African American women's leadership in the labor movement is most pronounced. In the context of the multicultural membership of some unions, women such as Sylvia Woods, in local education director of the International Ladies Garment Workers Union (ILGWU) in New York City, found ways to negotiate and medi-ate among different ethnic groups, especially between White and Black people. They used direct confrontation and negotiation with messages such as, "You don't have to love one another, but you [all] wanted decent wages, hours, con-ditions of work" to emphasize their mutual purposes (Jones, 1985, p. 252).

Like their counterparts in the North, southern Black women were active and vocal union organizers. Theodosia Simpson, a steam machine operator at the R. J. Reynolds Tobacco Company (RJR) in Winston-Salem, North Carolina, along with her co-workers, Velma Hopkins and Moranda Smith, quickly assumed leading roles in the June 1943 strike against RJR (Jones, 1985). They were noted for their willingness to confront personnel officials and take them to task on symbolic rhetoric designed to obfuscate wage issues. Smith eventually became

Southern Regional Director of the Food, Tobacco, Agricultural, and Allied Workers Union (FTA; Jones, 1985).

Women in the professions also exhibited leadership through organizing for change during this era, especially during World War II and the following decade. Their experiences demonstrate how an African American women's tradition of leadership as social justice and change was starting to take shape in the context of administration and management. For example, Dorothy Height is noted as the first African American woman on the inaugural committee (1942) of the Defense Advisory Committee on Women in the Services (DACOWITS; which included Mary Rockefeller and Mary Lord). She is also well-known for her leadership of the Young Women's Christian Association (YWCA), the National Council of Negro Women (NCNW), and Delta Sigma Theta sorority. Born in 1912, Height earned her bachelors and Master's degrees form New York University and did advanced study at Columbia University and the New York School of Social Work. By the late-1950s she was internationally known as an advocate and organizer for human rights and social justice. For instance in 1958 she was the YWCA representative at a 35-member Town Meeting of the World involving five Latin American countries. Also because of the leadership training programs she developed at the YWCA, she was sent to study the training needs of women's organizations in five West African countries (Hine, 1993).

Other women in the professions used voice strategies to work for social justice and change in their workplaces. For example, Charity Adams Early, the first African American woman to be commissioned as an officer in the Women's Arm Corps (WAC), spoke out against segregated recreational facilities and military housing in Europe and worked to improve conditions for women in the military (Hine, 1993). Similarly, Mabel Staupers organized a coordinated persuasive effort to eliminate quotas established by the U.S. Army Nurse Corps to limit the number of African American women who wanted to serve as nurses during WWII.

African American women in the professions found ways to negotiate and mediate among different groups—men, women, people of different races and nationalities—to affect change that affirmed the mutual purposes of those groups. It was an approach similar to the organizing tactics of African American women in working-class jobs, and it continued the traditions borne out of the experiences of enslaved African American women.

The Civil Rights Movement: African American Women's Leadership Tradition Crystallized

It is arguably in the context of the Civil Rights Movement that a tradition of African American women's leadership—grounded in a culture of resistance first forged in the era of slavery, and fine-tuned in the Black Women's Club Movement, other Black civic organizations, unions, and a general entrepreneurial spirit—begins to seem plausible. Several writers and participants in the movement emphasize that African American women were the invisible leaders of the movement (Aptheker, 1982; Hine & Thompson, 1998; Payne, 1995). In his important and well-documented book on the Mississippi freedom struggle of the early-1960s, Payne (1995) provided perhaps the most convincing evidence of the extraordinary influence of African American women's organizing traditions on the success of the early days of the movement. He documented the central role African American women played in leading, not just raising funds and handing out flyers. Because the voting rights campaign in Mississippi in 1962 brought together women and men of different races, religions, and ethnicities from across the country that had been working for social justice, it represents a microcosm of the grass roots organizing that characterized the early days of the Civil Rights Movement of the 1960s.

Payne's work raises two important issues that advance the argument for the existence of a tradition of African American women's leadership that crystallized in the Civil Rights Movement. First, he demonstrated that the women's (and men's) understanding of organizing and leadership appeared to be deeply entrenched in communal and family traditions that they themselves traced back to a tradition of resistance during the era of slavery. Indeed, Payne argued that a common thread among the organizers' family histories was a tradition of defiance, subtle or overt, that enabled a level of self-determination; "they were encouraged to believe that even within an oppressive social structure one retains some control over one's life" (Payne, 1995, p. 235).

Second, Payne (1995) highlighted the teaching and example of two African American women—Ella Jo Baker and Septima Clark—as exemplary of the kind of collective leadership that characterized the early days of the Civil Rights Movement. It was a kind of leadership that contrasted with a previously established leader-focused tradition reflected in the courageous work of Amzie Moore, Aaron Henry, and the martyred Medgar Evers, who tested the limits of repression in the era of Jim Crow in the 1940s and 1950s Mississippi. However, as activists began evolving a philosophy of leadership that focused on "the ability of the oppressed to participate in the reshaping of their own lives" (p. 68), Ella Baker and Septima Clark were primary in refining the principles of this kind of collective leadership (Payne, 1995). Here I profile the work of Ella Baker as a primary exemplar.

Ella Baker's Leadership: The Tradition Embodied. By many accounts, Ella Jo Baker was one of the major influences on the development of collective leadership practices in the early years of the Civil Rights Movement (Forman, 1985; Grant, 1998; Payne, 1995). Born in 1903, Ella Baker grew up in rural Virginia and North Carolina, raised in a family with explicit traditions of resistance and community activism (Grant, 1998; Payne, 1995). Over a period of about 30 years, from 1927 through 1960, she honed her own understanding of that tradition into an approach to leadership that emphasized the long-term development of leadership in ordinary women and men.

In 1927, shortly after graduating as valedictorian from Shaw University in Raleigh, North Carolina, Baker moved to New York City where, despite her college education, she could only find work as a waitress and a factory worker (Payne, 1995). However, she quickly became involved as an activist and organizer. By 1941, when she became Field Secretary for the NAACP, she was already a seasoned organizer, having been involved with the Harlem Adult Education Committee, the Workers' Education Movement and the Consumer Movement (aimed at organizing economic cooperatives during the Depression).

Through her work as NAACP Field Secretary, Baker began to set into motion her ideas about the "importance of organizing people to formulate their own questions, to define their own problems, and to find their own solutions" (Grant, 1998, p. 5). Critical of the rigid centralization of decision making at the national headquarters of the NAACP, she recognized that the challenge of organizing the huge mass base of the national organization (400,000 members by 1944) was in helping local branches identify and act on their local concerns. She traveled extensively through the South, "raising funds, organizing new branches, and trying to make old ones more effective" (Payne, 1995, p. 85). In 1943, when she became Director of Branches, she began organizing regional training programs and conferences for local leaders, putting into practice her ideas about leadership development in ordinary people. However, frustrated by the NAACP's resistance to democratization, Baker resigned her position as Director of Branches, but she continued her work in the Civil Rights Movement. She was one of the primary influences on the development of the Southern Christian Leadership Conference (SCLC), the organization formed after the pivotal Montgomery bus boycott, and eventually led by Dr. Martin Luther King, Jr.

Elected in 1957 as the SCLC's first full-time executive director, Baker attempted to incorporate her ideas about giving voice to the people through leadership development and organizing into its voter-registration and citizenship-training drives. However, she found the same resistance to democratizing that she experienced in the NAACP. For example she repeatedly pointed out the contradiction of "many SCLC preachers [that] would go out and give stirring speeches about human equality and then come back and treat the office staff as if they were personal servants" (Payne, 1995, p. 92).

Finally, in 1960, with the formation of the Student Nonviolent Coordinating Committee (SNCC, pronounced *snick*), Ella Baker was able to put her ideas about leadership into practice. Baker was instrumental in organizing SNCC from the corps of young people who were staging sit-ins to protest the (traditionally and legally) segregated lunch counters and public facilities across the country, including North Carolina, Tennessee, Alabama, and Virginia. SNCC was founded at the April 1960 conference that Baker organized at her alma mater, Shaw University. The conference brought together sit-in activists and leaders, including Dr. King and the Reverend James Lawson. However, it was Baker's understanding of grass roots organizing-as-leadership that transformed the early version of SNCC into a cutting-edge system for social change.

Baker's organizing-as-leadership approach reveals an organizing approach that brings together the foundations of a tradition of African American women's leadership. The central strategy was that of *collective leadership*, grounded in a theme of community building. Just as enslaved African American women combined an African heritage with American exigencies to forge networks of kin relations, and as 19th-century clubwomen sought to unite African American women in the rural and urban communities, Baker enacted a tradition that enabled people across class statuses, races, ages, religions, and ethnicities to identify with each other:

> You have to break that [inability to identify] down without alienating them at the same time. The gal who has been able to buy her minks and whose husband is a professional, they live well. You can't insult her, you never go and tell her she's a so-and-so for taking, for *not* identifying. You try to point where her interest lies in identifying with that other one across the tracks who doesn't have minks. (Payne, 1995, pp 88–89)

Baker's work reveals specific strategies for enacting collective leadership that are grounded in African American women's traditions of resistance and transformation. The first is *developing and using voice* (your own and others') as a mechanism to (a) invite participation in a collective effort and (b) work against the intrusions of hierarchy. As Baker (Payne, 1995) put it, "Everyone has a contribution to make. Just as one has to be able to look at a sharecropper and see a potential teacher, one most be able to look at a conservative lawyer and see a potential crusader for justice" (Payne, 1995, p. 89).

Marathon rap sessions, leader-training seminars (some were called, "Give the people the light, and they will come"), and more grass-roots oriented conferences were common mechanisms for surfacing potential contributions (Grant, 1998; Payne, 1995). One SNCC member, Courtland Cox, remembered one of the rap sessions in this way: "The most vivid memory I have of Ella Baker is of her sitting in those SNCC meetings that ran for days—you didn't measure them in hours, they ran days—with a smoke mask over her nose, listening patiently to words and discussions she must have heard a thousand times" (Payne, 1995, p. 97). Baker suggested institutionalizing listening into the highly formalized annual conferences that brought together members of the organizing effort. She designed a structure so that instead of staff members making speeches, several delegates [from local branches] were designated to talk out of their branch experiences (Payne, 1995). SNCC's unofficial slogan was "do what the people say do" (former member Julian Bond in Grant, 1998, p. xvi).

Another aspect of using voice to invite participation exemplified in Baker's leadership is speaking up when the collective effort is being compromised. This philosophy was especially useful within the context of entrenched bureaucracy that characterized aspects of many institutions integral to the movement, including the church, the SCLC, and the NAACP. Baker consistently pointed out the contradictions in the fact that "Many SCLC preachers could go out and give stirring speeches about human equality and come back and treat the office staff as if they were personal servants" (Payne, 1995, p. 92). Former SNCC member, Julian Bond, noted that Baker "was never able to convince the New York headquarters to listen to the voices of members of the field.... But she did manage to touch the lives of thousands, ingraining her suspicion of hierarchies and her faith in democracy—always with a lowercase 'd'" (Grant, 1998, p. xvi).

A final strategy emphasized self-definition and self-determination as a basis for long-term development of leadership in ordinary men and women. In the context of Baker's approach to social change, self-definition, and self-determination was a form of self-promotion that paradoxically advanced the common good. She accomplished this through a variety of mechanisms that emphasized creating opportunities for people to speak from their own experiences, and giving them support to implement their ideas. For example, she advocated creating regional offices of the NAACP so that local leaders would have a source of assistance nearer than New York. She advocated having small groups of people maintain effective working relationships among themselves, "but also retaining contact in some form with other such cells, so that coordinated action would be possible whenever large numbers really were necessary" (Payne, 1995, p. 94).

Although I emphasize Ella Baker's work as embodying an African American women's leadership tradition during the Civil Rights Movement, countless other women exemplified this kind of collective leadership. Much of the leadership work was completed through adult-education programs conducted in churches, community centers, and homes, in conjunction with organizations such as The Highlander Folk School, Citizenship Schools, Fellowship of Reconciliation, the NAACP, the Urban League, Congress of Racial Equality, and The

Mississippi Freedom Democratic Party (Gyant, 1990; Payne, 1995). The educational programs emerging from these organizations were designed:

> to teach adults how to read and write so that they could pass the literacy test to become registered voters ... [and] to provide other training to give African Americans the opportunity to become active participants in the political, social, educational, and economical spheres in this country. (Gyant, 1990, p. 4)

Septima Clark, Daisy Bates, Rosa Parks, and Fannie Lou Hammer are women noted in published historical accounts whose work demonstrated this tradition of leadership. Other work was done by hundreds of women who were active in their communities.

As mentioned, several writers and participants in the movement emphasize that African American women were leaders of the movement (Aptheker, 1982; Hine & Thompson, 1995; Payne, 1995). These were women of different class statuses and geographic locations that seldom spoke to the press or got their picture in the paper but, in fact, were disproportionately involved in the day-to-day activities of the early civil rights struggle. In line with my argument, Hine and Thompson argued that African American women's history of participation in community activities and their cultural preparation for resistance account for their important leadership role in the Civil Rights Movement.

Two important questions remain, however. First, to what extent is a tradition of leadership revealed in contemporary African American women's experiences? Second, how is it manifested in the context of 21st-century organizational leadership? I address these questions in the third and final part of this volume.

ENDNOTE

1. Perhaps the most comprehensive chronicle of African American women's achievements is Hine's (1993) two-volume set, *Black Women in America: An Historical Encyclopedia.* Brooklyn, NY: Carlson.

III

African American Women Executives and 21st-Century Organizational Leadership: Deconstructing "Masculine" and "Feminine" Leadership, Embracing Duality in Leadership Practice

Part III brings together the major themes of this book, demonstrating that the leadership traditions revealed in the history of Black women in America are exemplified in contemporary African American women's leadership approaches. Drawing upon case studies of 15 African American women executives who came of age during the era of the Civil Rights and feminist movements of the 1960s and 1970s, I demonstrate how these traditions can inform leadership in the context of 21st-century organizations. The contemporary vision of organizational leadership that emerges from the women's experiences disrupts traditional *masculine* and *feminine* notions of leadership and other leadership dualisms, and shifts the focus to a both/and approach to leadership practice in the era of postindustrialization and globalization.

CULTURAL TRADITIONS OF RESISTANCE
AND CHANGE: FOCUSING ON CONTEMPORARY
AFRICAN AMERICAN WOMEN
AS ORGANIZATIONAL LEADERS

The leadership traditions revealed in the history of Black women in America are exemplified in the experiences of the women executives who participated in this research. The focus on African American women in management (as opposed to women at various levels of the organization) is intended as a counter narrative to the gender and leadership studies that focus almost exclusively on White women in management. Although recently, some scholars have studied African American women in management, they have not emphasized leadership as a primary focus (see Bell & Nkomo, 2001; Etter-Lewis, 1993; Nkomo, 1992; Thomas & Gabarro, 1996). Similar to much of the research on organizational leadership, these works focus on management as opposed to leadership (Rost, 1991), and tend to center on career advancement in the corporate sector. However in this book, I focus on African American women's tradition of leadership in the context of formal organizations.

The personal histories of each of the women reveal the influence of their mothers, fathers, "othermothers," and contemporary and ancestral others in their extended families and communities that strengthened their identity as Black women and that influenced their approaches to leadership (Parker, 1997). The recurring theme across the women's narratives—whether they were born into working class or middle- and upper class families—was "Don't forget where you came from," referring to the history of struggle, survival, and triumph in African American experience. I quote two examples at length, to emphasize the salience of the women's narratives in creating their sense of tradition and leadership.

One executive, the senior administrator for a large federal government agency, described how traditions from her Black upper class family instilled in her the traditions of religion and service to the community:

> There is so much unspoken. I knew that we were special. I knew that we were different. I knew that we had advantage, but with awareness of whatever this specialness was, came the obligation to do for and to give to and support others, especially in education. Very traditional family with strong roots to the church and public activism. My grandfather was a physician. My grandmother on that side, my maternal grandmother, had the distinction of helping to build public support for the first public library for Negroes, as we were then called.... So, the family tradition was of leadership and also a great sense of responsibility for the broader community. I have recollection of [my maternal] grandmother whose back porch was always filled with clothing, clean, folded clothing in sizes that she routinely gave to others.... And she was always identifying people, some of whom were in her employ, worked in her res-

taurant, who needed help. She brought thirteen of her relatives out of that almost plantation-like environment in southwest Virginia, to see them educated as well. And so, that's sort of the tradition of the family.

Emphasizing more recent family history, another executive, director of a major revenue generating division of a national communications company, told the story of how her parents instilled in her the courage to confront systems of oppression, even if it meant standing alone:

> My parents were always involved and they were always committed to making a difference. I say that because I can remember at a very young age my mother and father were involved in the Civil Rights Movement. I always knew my parents were not afraid. They were never afraid of leadership. They were never afraid of taking a difficult stand ... I think that is what definitely probably developed most of my personality. When I was in the second grade they sent me to a school that at the time was predominantly White and by that I mean there was two Blacks, me and my next door neighbor. It was *way* before [schools were legally integrated] ... and so they always stepped out ahead and made me do the difficult thing for whatever reason. They had to write letters and had to, you know, they had to go through a bunch of mess, but I mean of course they couldn't keep us out.... And I remember crying and being very upset and telling my mother I don't want to be going to a White school. My mother said, "Don't worry; it's not White it's red brick." And so that kind of helped shape my ideas. You know, in terms of it's okay to stand alone. It's okay to do the difficult thing because, you know, this is life. So that's the leadership thing for me.

Even with the diversity in geographic location and socioeconomic status, there are striking similarities in the ways these executives learned leadership and, subsequently, the ways in which they enact leadership within dominant culture organizations. This reinforces an organic view of Black culture providing the threads that tie the women's experiences together. In recounting their life histories, the executives emphasized the inner strength and knowledge they gained through the messages and interpersonal influence from their parents and other significant adults in their lives. These messages and sources of influence served as a powerful force that helped them meet successfully the challenges and opportunities they encountered throughout their careers, and that strengthened their capacities for leadership.

21st-Century Organizations as a Context for African American Women's Leadership Traditions: Illuminating the Centrality of Race in Organizing

I argue that the context from which African American women's leadership traditions emerged is one that necessitated creating community, embracing change, and resisting ideological domination, in a multicultural, fragmented, and power-based social world. These same conditions are recreated in the postindustrial workplace, where identities and relationships are not fixed but must be negotiated in a social world that is for everyone—people of both sexes and of different gender identities, ethnicities, races, classes, sexual orientations—increasingly fragmented and disconnected (Fairclough, 1992; Giddens, 1991). The postindustrial workplace is increasingly fragmented, multicultural and fundamentally raced, gendered, and classed (Parker, 2003).

Yet, as Prasad, Mills, Elmes, and Prasad (1997) argued, organizations continue to advance and value *monoculturalism*, even as there is an emphasis on *multiculturalism* through diversity initiatives. Prasad et al. reviewed the vast literature on workplace diversity, focusing on a number of different dimensions, such as gender, race, ethnicity, migrancy and immigration, colonialism, and globalization. They concluded that despite the proliferation of research on discrimination, the value of diversity, and multiculturalism in organizations, the literature fails to address the more serious dimensions of difference in organizations (vs. Allen, 2004). The authors contend that a host of gender conflicts, race tensions, and cultural frictions lie hidden in the shadows of the elaborate showcasing of the diversity movement.

Focusing on African American women executives' experiences negotiating their identities within raced and gendered interaction contexts reveals some insights about race tensions and cultural frictions in the contemporary workplace. As reported in a previous analysis of data from this study, the women perceived challenges related to their identity as Black women in two salient interaction contexts: interacting with their White male executive peers, and interacting with African American co-workers and clients (Parker, 2002). In both these contexts the conflicts centered on perceived expectations about the relationship and the women's identity as African American women. Salient conflicts involving White male peers centered on the issue of inclusiveness or fit. The women perceived that their colleagues' unspoken assumptions about their presence as African American women in a traditionally White male setting sometimes reinforced patterns of interaction that challenged or undermined the women's authority. The women understood these instances as misguided assumptions that simply needed to be set straight. In more theoretical terms, their colleagues' actions might be viewed as structured by a system that reproduces monoculturalism. The men themselves may have been committed to diversity at the executive level, but their interaction with the women was influenced by established patterns of raced and gendered discourses that shaped the way they responded.

It was the African American women who were instrumental in expressing the struggle, identifying and defining perceptions of the salient elements of the conflict, and ensuring a negotiated resolution. This reinforces the importance of centering marginalized voices as a way of disrupting discourses that exclude rather than invite participation. Significantly, the women's White male colleagues, unaware of how their own interaction might be perceived as contributing to creating the conflict, were positioned to avoid such self-reflection and intellectual work. However, in the instances reported by the women in this study, the men willingly engaged in the process once it was brought to the foreground (Parker, 2002).

Similarly perceived problematic interactions between the executives and other African Americans both inside and outside the organization are influenced by larger cultural discursive texts. Focusing on the sociohistorical context that gave rise to racial solidarity as one response to oppressive structures in U.S. American society, race can be seen as a way of structuring interactions between and among African Americans in dominant culture organizations, forcing them into dualistic discourses of Black nationalism or assimilationism, or being Black-identified or White-identified. The women expressed a degree of ambivalence about their strategies for managing the conflict, yet they seemed fully aware of the salience of intraracial differences in the contemporary workplace. This ambivalence can be interpreted as indicative of an ongoing process among African Americans in general and African American women in particular, for rearticulating the basis for collective bonding (hooks, 1990).

The emphasis on monoculturalism in the workplace presumes an absence of racial, gender, and class conflict (Prasad et al., 1997). Yet the accounts of raced and gendered interaction experiences from African American women executives in this study reveal that, as workforce diversity increases, there is a need for processes that help organizational members work through the politics and contradictions of their own background experiences, identity, and preconceived notions as they encounter others who are different. The purpose of leadership in such a context is to facilitate dialogue in which each person is empowered to resist domination and oppression, as she or he comes to understand the contribution they can make, if any, to what they perceive as the collective endeavor of organizing. I argue that African American women's traditions of leadership and organizing provide a way of envisioning this process.

The following chapters present a re-envisioning of leadership conceptualized from the standpoints of the African American women executives who participated in this study. It is based on the ideas that African American women's approaches to leadership (a) emerge from a particular way of viewing complex, often contradictory, life experiences; and (b) provide an exemplar of a meaning-centered approach to leadership in 21st-century organizations that deconstructs traditional notions of masculine and feminine leadership. In these chapters, I target central dualistic notions that lie at the heart of traditional, Western (White middle class) notions of feminine versus masculine leadership: instrumentality versus collaboration and control versus empowerment. In so doing, I shift the focus to a both/and approach that captures some of the tensions and paradoxes in the leadership process.

5

Re-Envisioning Instrumentality
as Collaboration

This chapter presents an overview of the leadership approach derived from case studies of 15 African American women executives and their co-workers. In total, the leadership communication themes revealed in this study challenge the dichotomous notions of instrumentality and collaboration advanced in the gender and leadership literature. This chapter provides a brief overview of each of the themes and how they inform an approach to leadership that disrupts traditional masculine and feminine models. Then, in Chapter 6, I discuss the themes in more detail, including the voices of the executives and their coworkers. In both chapters, I show how the women's leadership communication represents a meaning-centered approach that emphasizes both individual and relational (systems) concerns (Fairhurst, 2001).

As mentioned in Chapter 2, two competing leadership models are advanced—masculine instrumentality versus feminine collaboration—based almost exclusively on studies of White women and men but presented as racially and culturally neutral (Parker & ogilvie, 1996). The masculine model of leadership is theorized as representative of *male values*, such as distance and detachment (Marshall, 1993), and men are said to be socialized to use instrumental communication—unilateral, directive and aimed at controlling others—which is consistent with their learned view of talk as a way to assert self and achieve status (Eagly & Karau, 1991). Common symbolic representations of the masculine leadership model include characteristics such as aggressiveness, independence, risk-taking, rationality, and intelligence (Collins, 1998b; Connell, 1995).

The feminine model of leadership is associated with *female values*, such as nurturance and support (Marshall, 1993) and are thought to be a reflection of traditionally defined White middle-class women's socialized patterns of collaborative communication (Helgesen, 1990, Lunneborg, 1990; Rosener, 1990). Common symbolic representations of this model include characteristics such as nurturance, compassion, sensitivity to others' needs, and caring (Collins, 1998b; Grant, 1988).

Universalizing masculine and feminine models of leadership based on Western (White-middle and upper-class) gendered identities excludes the experiences of other groups and renders them nonlegitimate or peripheral in the production of knowledge. It also "dangerously romanticizes women's values, the family, the separation of 'domestic' and 'public' spheres ... and the interplay of family dynamics and legal systems to challenge these images of male and female" (Calàs & Smircich, 1996, p. 241). More generally, these competing models unnecessarily reinforce dualistic thinking about leadership, obscuring the meanings, tensions, and paradoxes of leadership as it is realized in practice (Fairhurst, 2001). The findings of this study challenge these trends by deconstructing and presenting a revision of traditional notions of instrumentality and collaboration.

OVERVIEW OF AFRICAN AMERICAN WOMEN EXECUTIVES' LEADERSHIP APPROACHES

Five themes related to leadership communication were revealed in the interviews and observations of the 15 African American women executives and their co-workers that participated in this study. The themes are: (a) interactive communication; (b) empowerment through the challenge to produce results; (c) openness in communication; (d) participative decision making through collaborative debate, autonomy, and information gathering; and (e) leadership through boundary spanning (see Table 5.1).

Interactive Communication

This theme represents the central dimension of the African American women executives' leadership because it forms the basis of their overall approach to communicating leadership. The women's leadership can be characterized as interactive in both a theoretical and relational sense. In the theoretical sense, the women's leadership emphasizes interaction of both individual and systems concerns. They are very much involved in negotiating the space between employees' needs and values and organizational needs and values. The women's leadership is

TABLE 5.1
African American Women Executive Study Participants

	Executive Title	Industry	Public/Private
1	Vice President, Administrative Services	Insurance	Private
2	Vice President, Marketing	Computer	Private
3	Vice President, Operations	Communications	Private
4	General Manager	Communications	Private
5	Area Manager	Communications	Private
6	Vice President, Marketing	Insurance	Private
7	Area Manager	Communications	Private
8	Financial Officer	Communications	Private
9	Director	State Government	Public
10	Officer	Federal Government	Public
11	Vice Chair	Political Party	Public
	Mayor	City Government	Public
12	Associate Superintendent	Education	Public
13	Director	City Government	Public
14	Officer/Director	Federal Government State Government	Public
15	Director	State Government	Public

also interactive in the relational sense. That is, all the executives placed a high premium on oral communication for creating and sustaining relationships. Their leadership is practiced primarily through face-to-face interaction.

However, none of the executives are micromanagers who insist on having tight control over employee activities. Instead the data revealed an interactive leadership approach reminiscent of the traditions supporting self-definition and self-determination in African American women's history. Three themes elaborate the interactive approach as facilitating both personal and organizational growth and learning: (a) knowing the business, its mission, and its goals, and being able to communicate that knowledge clearly, directly, and consistently; (b) being accessible to staff and customers; and (c) modeling effective behavior The women and their co-workers presented an image of the executives as a kind of conduit through which organizational members could determine courses of action, hash out concerns, identify their own successes, and help bring about needed changes.

Empowerment of Employees Through the Challenge to Produce Results

From the perspective of these executives, a key tool for motivating employees is expecting high performance, based on the executive's confidence in the person's ability to deliver and then setting specific goals for producing high-quality results. This approach informs a strategy for empowerment that is *simultaneously* directive (e.g., transmission centered) and nondirective (e.g., emergent or meaning centered). It is directive in the sense that there is a clearly initiated structure; it is nondirective in that the employees are encouraged to exercise a great deal of freedom within the initiated structure, and indeed to change the structure if they see fit. Employee descriptions of this approach as a form of empowerment provide persuasive evidence of its value.

Openness in Communication

The third leadership theme emerged from descriptions of the executives as direct communicators. *Directness* is a label that is often associated with African American women's communication (McGoldrick, Garcia-Preto, Hines, & Lee, 1988). In the larger historical cultural context that devalues African American women, having a direct communication style is seen as negative, reflecting stereotypes of the *Black Matriarch* or *Sapphire*. Contemporary studies show that Whites generalized perceptions of African American women's communication style are negative (Kochman, 1981; Weitz & Gordon, 1993). However, as revealed in this study, perceptions of African American women's communication in actual interaction reveal a more positive view of directness. From the standpoint of the women and their co-workers, directness as a form of leadership communication style was interpreted positively. Here, directness means (a) bringing important issues into the open, (b) making sure voices (including their own) that need to be heard on a certain issue get that opportunity, and (c) having no hidden agendas. The data revealed that this directness through openness is accomplished not only at the interpersonal level but also at the group and organizational levels.

Participative Decision Making Through Collaborative Debate, Autonomy, and Information Gathering

The fourth theme emphasizes employee empowerment and community building through participative decision-making practices. The data revealed that all the executives used some form of participative decision making. Similar to the emphases on building community in historical traditions of African American women's leadership, the women used personal involvement and attention as a medium for initiating structure, identifying places of struggle or conflicting viewpoints, and encouraging autonomy and self-definition. Specifically, the women used a combination of three tactics to facilitate participative decision making: collaborative debate, autonomy, and information gathering. Several of them used a *collaborative debate* structure. The term *collaborative debate* is used to refer to the process of dialectic inquiry in which employees who are likely to disagree with prevailing opinions are invited to give input via one-to-one argument and explicit agreement and refutation (Kennedy, 1980) for the purpose of collaboratively reaching decisions. This might involve bringing together diverse or conflicting groups or simply pulling together the groups necessary to move forward on a project that had been stifled by indecision and disagreement.

Decision autonomy is another decision participation tactic revealed in the data. Employee accounts showed evidence that the executives encouraged departments to be autonomous in making decisions, for example, "bringing the executive in the loop," as one employee phrased it, "only when they needed to."

The third tactic for inviting participation is information gathering, with emphasis placed on assembling experiences and knowledge dispersed throughout the organizational unit. The women saw themselves as a conduit through which the diversity of viewpoints could be brought together, negotiated, and enacted, and their employees confirmed this viewpoint.

Leadership Through Boundary Spanning

The women's leadership communication revealed a re-envisioning of fixed organizational boundaries as permeable and fluid enactments of conversation and community building. According to the executives' supervisors interviewed, women were effective in articulating the organization's mission and purpose and connecting the organization to the community in positive ways. These connections reveal an approach to leadership, reminiscent of the kind of community building in African American women's history, where it is possible to redefine a community based on a pressing need.

DECONSTRUCTING "TRADITIONAL" NOTIONS OF INSTRUMENTALITY AND COLLABORATION

Taken together, these themes challenge traditional notions of instrumental leadership as *directive and controlling,* and collaborative leadership as *nurturing and caring.* This study revealed an approach to leadership where collaboration is worked out at the intersections of control and empowerment. *Control* is (re)defined as interactive and personal, rather than as competitive and distant, and becomes a means for empowerment. The leader's focus is on the other, not as a means of affirming the other person, per se—although that may be a likely outcome—but as a way of assessing points of view and levels of (others' as well as their own) readiness to perform.

Redefining Instrumentality

Instrumentality as a leadership strategy is often characterized as direct—unilateral, competitive, and aimed at controlling others—consistent with traditional views of White, middle-class masculine communication patterns (Eagly, 1987; Rosener, 1990). In this study, African American women executives' communication is described as direct, but the interpretations are positive and proactive. Grounded in the experiences of the executives and the people with whom they interact, the notion of directness is (re)defined as a type of openness in communication designed to invite dialogue and personal growth.

This view reconceptualizes instrumentality as both direct and relational (Fairhurst, 2001). It is direct, in terms of the strategic framing and transmission of messages (Fairhurst & Saar, 1996), and relational, in terms of the emphasis on dialogue and meaning construction. This view broadens the concept of instrumentality to include processes associated with transformational leadership—charisma, inspiration, providing intellectual stimulation, and showing individualized consideration (Avolio & Bass, 1988; Bass, 1985). Additionally, with the dual emphasis on strategic message transmission and dialogue, this expanded view of instrumentality casts both leaders and followers as active agents in the creation of organizational meaning.

Redefining Collaboration

In this study, *collaboration* is revealed as a negotiated and dynamic process that combines redefined elements of instrumentality, control, and empowerment. As a leadership strategy, this view of collaboration emphasizes the paradoxical practice of direct engagement (i.e., constraint/structure) that creates routes for individual empowerment and community building (i.e., creativity/process). It contradicts the *either–or* thinking of traditional notions of collaboration and instrumentality and more accurately captures the *both/and* nature of organizational leadership (Fairhurst, 2000; Marshall, 1993). African American women executives' interactive approach to leadership provides a way for leaders in an increasingly diverse workplace to serve as conduits through which a diversity of viewpoints can be brought together, negotiated, and enacted.

Disrupting Traditional Views of "Feminine" and "Masculine" Leadership

This view challenges the symbolic images of women as master collaborators who shun attempts to control others (Helgesen, 1990; Loden, 1985). Rather than viewing collaboration as an *alternative* to control, where control is defined in terms of traditionally *masculine* values such as distance, detachment and inviting competition (Marshall, 1993), *directness* and *control* are a means for collaboration. *Control* is redefined as personal and interactive. The focus is on the other, as a way of assessing points of view and levels of readiness to perform.

The (re)conceptualized notions of collaboration and instrumentality reported in this study counters the hegemonic discourses that have suppressed Black women's ideas and expands traditional views of organizational leadership. By placing Black women at the center of analysis, we can begin to see the both/and quality of Black women's voices (Collins, 1990). Behavior deemed as controlling, conflictual, or acquiescent through a larger cultural text that devalues African American women, is understood here as the capacity for African American women to see the infinite possibilities of individual characteristics through a lens of constructing a solution. Emerging from a social location at the intersection of race, gender, and class oppression within dominant culture society, African American women's voices are simultaneously confrontational (in response to different interests) and collaborative (in response to shared interests, Collins, 1998a). The result is a process of leadership that produces what Collins termed "contextualized truth." Based on Mae Henderson's (1989) metaphor of "speaking in tongues," contextualized truth emerges through the interaction of logic, creativity, and accessibility" (Collins, 1998a, p. 239). Implicit in the process of producing contextualized truth is the willingness and ability to construe knowledge and values from multiple perspectives without loss of commitment to one's own values (Bruner, 1990, p. 30).

In the next chapter, I elaborate on this view of African American women's organizational leadership as a process for producing contextualized truth. I discuss the leadership themes from the study in more detail, including the voices of the executives and their co-workers to show how the women's leadership communication represents a meaning centered approach that emphasizes both individual and relational (systems) concerns (Fairhurst, 2001). In so doing, I shift the focus to a both/and approach that captures some of the tensions and paradoxes in the leadership process.

6

Embracing Duality
in Leadership Practice:
Re-Envisioning Control
as Empowerment
and Community Building

This chapter details the leadership approach derived from the study of African American women executives and their coworkers, that exemplifies the meaning-centered view of leadership described in chapter 2. Using a critical feminist lens, I combine two meaning-centered views to define leadership in the following way: "Leadership is an influence relationship among leaders and followers who intend real changes that reflect their mutual purposes" (Rost, 1991, p. 102); [and these mutual purposes are negotiated through a process] "whereby one or more individuals [leaders and followers] succeeds in attempting to frame and define the reality of others" (Smircich & Morgan, 1982, p. 258).

This view shifts attention toward leadership as a process focused on emancipation and change, and emphasizing the mutual influence of both leaders and followers in a flow of contested and negotiated meaning production. How this process unfolds is the focus of this chapter.

The view of leadership revealed in this study takes into account the complexities, tensions, and contradictions inherent in the leadership process. The leadership communication themes challenge the central conflict in the industrial versus postindustrial views of leadership—control versus empowerment. It presents a view of control as a means for empowerment and collaboration, where control is redefined as personal and interactive, rather than as distant and competitive. This view of leadership suggests a process dependent simultaneously on follower autonomy and direct leader engagement and responsiveness.

INTERACTIVE LEADERSHIP

This theme represents the central dimension of the African American women executives' leadership approach because it forms the basis of their overall approach to communicating leadership (see Table 6.1). The women's leadership can be characterized as interactive, meaning that they are very much involved in negotiating the space between employees' needs and values and organizational needs and values. And they do this by creating opportunities for negotiating meanings in relational contexts. Their leadership is practiced primarily through face-to-face interaction, characterized by the following subthemes: (a) knowing the business, its mission, and its goals, and being able to communicate that knowledge clearly, directly, and consistently; (b) being accessible to staff and customers; and (c) modeling effective behavior. Each of these subthemes represents a form of leadership intended to facilitate both personal and organizational growth and learning within a context of change and contested meanings.

Communicating Knowledge About the Business

One way the executives demonstrated interactive leadership was through knowing the business, its mission, and its goals, and being able to communicate that knowledge in ways that directly engaged employees, clients, and other organizational constituents. One executive, who had left her post in senior management just prior to the interview, described her strategy for communicating her vision in this way:

> I was always out there painting my vision. I was really talking to people. I managed, if you will, by walking around. You know, whatever their piece was, I really went to paint the vision for them of what their piece contributed to our getting up here. Let's say the clerks that answered the phone. I told them, "You're the ears for this entire [organization]. People call in and talk to you, and if you don't make them feel that they're wonderful, then they start talking about how horrible we are. They don't remember what I am or what I do ... It's you." And then all of a sudden they start feeling, "Well our job is the most important job in the [organization]."

Similarly, another executive says she coaches her employees on how to communicate about the business:

TABLE 6.1
Overview of African American Women Executives'
Leadership Communication

Leadership Communication Theme	Description
Interactive Leadership	• Knowing the business, its mission, and its goals, and being able to communicate that knowledge clearly, directly, and consistently • Being accessible to staff and customers • Modeling effective behavior
Empowerment of Employees Through the Challenge to Produce Results	• Expecting high performance, based on the executive's confidence in the person's ability to deliver • Setting specific goals for producing high quality results
Openness in Communication	• Bringing important issues into the open • Making sure voices (including their own) that need to be heard on a certain issue get that opportunity • Having no hidden agendas
Participative Decision Making	• Collaborative Debate: Dialectic inquiry that involves one-to-one argument and explicit agreement and refutation for the purpose of collaboratively reaching decisions • Autonomy: Trusting employees and pushing control of the organization to the lowest levels • Information Gathering: Staying aware of multiple points of views
Leadership Through Boundary Spanning Communication	• Connecting the organization to the community in positive ways • Articulating the organization's mission and purpose.

One of the things that I told my managers in some meetings, months ago [was] ... when somebody asks you how's it going, you tell them "Great! This month, my group alone contributed $320,000 to the market area!" or "So far this year, our whole office has already done 4.3 million dollars for the company!" And, so, I said that's the only thing people really respect, is numbers, dollars, and what is going on. And so, it's how you present it in a positive way. If you're like well you know, we've got some people who aren't coming to work on time. So what. The point is most [units] in this company don't generate money. They do servicing. They make sure the [services] are O.K. You've got to have those, those organizations so that you can sell and so that you can get things in. But, I'm like, "You need to be proud. Hey, you are generating money for the company." ... When I was in external affairs I didn't generate money for the company. I gave money away. But I didn't generate it.

By engaging employees directly and frequently about their vision, the executives served as an important reference point for interpreting the organization's goals. One staff member commented:

[S]he is very good at molding her vision and goals into most all of her communications, whether they be one-on-one, whether they be group discussions with small groups, or in general communications with the organization as a whole ... [S]he has an ability to fold [her vision and goals] in and keep them out front and visible to everybody so they always have that longer term sight of what those goals are.

One measure of effectiveness in communicating an organizational vision is consistency among organizational leaders and their followers in articulating a vision as it relates to the organizational mission and goals (Schein, 1991). In this study, I observed high consistency among the executives and their staff in the descriptions of the organizational mission and goals.

Accessibility

Another expression of the interactive leadership theme is accessibility. Several of the direct reports described their executive as approachable and as a good listener, revealing an overall tendency toward accessible leadership. For example, one staff member gave this account to describe her executive's approachability and listening effectiveness:

Her calendar is usually really, really tight, but she makes it a point that once she's out there she comes and personally interacts with the service reps, gets to know who they are ... I'll give you an example ... [O]ne of my reps and her sister [were] in another office and [had] been trying to transfer [here]. And, this young lady walked up to [the executive] and she said, "Oh hi, I understand I just got my transfer, I'm over here now." And [the executive] said "great, great!" She goes, "And you know, I'm still trying to get my sister over here." Well, [the executive] came to my area last week, and she walked up to her and said "Hi, [says the employee's name correctly] right? Listen, any luck getting your sister here yet?" She said, "As a matter of fact, yes, her transfer just came through," And [the executive] said "Oh great!" So, people know that [the executive] communicates with them, because she listens to what they say.... So I think people see how hard she works, and they work just as hard. I think, it's, you know, leadership by example.

The executives themselves viewed modeling effective behavior as central to their leadership approach. One executive explained how behavior modeling serves as a powerful motivational tool:

> So my leadership style is personal involvement. Earlier this year I felt that my sales teams needed additional sales training. I personally ... found a consultant, met with the consultant, told him what I wanted him to do in the class. The first class [I attended] with my managers. I said, "I'm going to take this class. Y'all better show up. It's going to start on Sunday afternoon and it's going to go through Friday." I was there. And I stayed in the class the entire six days, which means, "You can't walk out of this class. If I'm in here and you're not in the classroom ... I'm going, 'Well, I guess you don't need this, huh?'" I get directly involved with them. I don't ask them to do anything I won't do. I didn't ask my managers to go to the class if I wasn't going to go to the class.

Collectively, the descriptions informing the interactive leadership theme reveal an emphasis on personal involvement that reinterprets the notion of control as interactive and personal rather than as distant and competitive. The executives' interactive style of control does not stifle employee autonomy. Indeed, staff members talked about feeling quite autonomous and even empowered as a result of their executive's interactive leadership approach. This process of empowerment points to the second theme related to the African American women executives' leadership approach.

EMPOWERMENT OF EMPLOYEES THROUGH THE CHALLENGE TO PRODUCE RESULTS

From the perspective of these executives, a key tool for motivating employees is expecting high performance, based on the executive's confidence in the person's ability to deliver, and then setting specific goals for producing high-quality results. This approach informs a strategy for empowerment that is *simultaneously* directive and nondirective. It is directive in the sense that there is a clearly initiated structure within which employees are expected to operate; and it is nondirective in that the employees are encouraged to exercise a great deal of freedom within the initiated structure. The most persuasive evidence of employee empowerment is provided by staff comments. For example, one staff member commented:

> I think when she has trust in a person's substantive knowledge and judgment, she, you know, wants you to be out there doing what she thinks you would want her to do [needs to be done].... She's very focused; never wants to have a meeting for the sake of the meeting. Wants an outcome on everything that happens.

Wants assignments to come out of there. Wants people to come back with their assignments done. For example, during meetings, she turns to her staff and says, "You own that; that's your responsibility; do it." Every meeting that's what happens. [And if, for some reason, someone doesn't own a task effectively], she will get on the phone and say, "You haven't delivered." She believes in interacting directly with people.

Along similar lines, another executive's staff member commented:

I think she's very people oriented, but understanding that, she also wants action. She wants things moving in a positive direction. She's not happy with status quo, as I told you before. But she balances it with the people, you know, she's very caring to the people. [The executive] looks out for our best interest. But understand that people know that if they're not accountable, she will step up to doing what she needs to do. I mean, there is no question. She holds people accountable ... if you're not doing your job, you may not be here.

In addition to the staff members' accounts, the executives' supervisors also commented about empowering employees through the challenge to perform. One executive's supervisor said:

I think she's very direct. I think if you talk to the people who work in the organization, it is all business. That doesn't translate to any lack of humanism ... I think she is very compassionate. She really goes to bat for people, particularly if she believes that they're trying to improve and that they're working hard at it. I think she's going to drive and lead and expect, you know, people to perform. On the other hand, everybody is not at the same place at the same time. And it's okay to struggle, and you don't have to be at the same place at the same time, but you had better be improving. And she's not sympathetic for someone who's less than committed.

Indeed the executives themselves described their approach to developing employees in terms of empowerment through encouraging autonomy.

What stands out among these accounts is the paradoxical notion that the employees feel a sense of autonomy that is, to a certain extent, mandated by the executive. Tensions reproduced by this paradox of structure (Stohl & Cheney, 2001) are managed by communication practices that emphasize a kind of openness that is redefined from Black women's standpoints.

OPENNESS IN COMMUNICATION

The third leadership theme emerged from descriptions of the executives as direct communicators. Data from the executives' staff members and supervisors revealed words and phrases such as *direct, straightforward, shoots it straight, de-*

manding, all business precise, focused, and *dynamic* to describe the women's leadership. Moreover, each of the executives described herself in terms such as *direct, to the point, opinionated,* or *focused.* When asked to elaborate on these words or phrases, the interpretation of directness that emerged was openness in communication not meant to intimidate, but to negotiate.

Directness is a label that is often associated with African American women's communication (McGoldrick, Garcia-Preto, Hines, & Lee, 1988), although the interpretation is often negative (Hecht, Ribeau, & Roberts, 1989; Kochman, 1981; Shuter & Turner, 1997; Ting-Toomey, 1986; Weitz & Gordon, 1993). From the standpoint of these African American women executives and their co-workers, directness is interpreted positively. Here, directness means (a) bringing important issues into the open, (b) making sure voices (including their own) that need to be heard on a certain issue get that opportunity, and (c) having no hidden agendas. The data revealed that this directness through openness is accomplished not only at the interpersonal level, but also at the group and organizational levels as well. Here is how one executive described her strategy for raising important issues and getting the 140,000 members of her organization involved in a dialogue that created their strategic mission:

> It is very important to get everybody [in the entire organization] clear ... to get everybody focused on what we do. And people were unclear about what we did. You know, people who worked in [one particular] program thought we do [goals connected to that specific program]. But they didn't see their ties to the [core activities of the organization]. The people [in] another area of emphasis had their own mission statement], but they didn't see their tie to the heart and soul of us.... It was very important, once again, to have everybody in, you know, my universe of some 140,000 people understand that [there is a common mission]. So I have worked very hard to engage people for almost nine months so that [everyone who is a part of the organization] ... and I've got Nobel Prize laureates who work for me, and sometimes they don't think so—but to engage them in this debate as we shape where we are going for the twenty-first century. So I took a hundred leaders in the organization, union, non-union, labs—each one of these ... probably these people didn't know what the other guy did. And we banged away at it for three and a half days. They went off to their various complexes. We came back six months later and came up with, you know, this [pictorial model that symbolizes] ... "This is what we do, and this is what we do in the face of the [current environment]. So I had used this concept of trying to show where the interconnections are. So, then that led to an expression of our core values, which really tied to customer service and valuing others to trying to express our mission so everybody understands it, to this iteration of what drives us.

The pictorial model the executive described was displayed prominently in the foyer of her office and served as a symbol of the executive's style of open engagement. Approaching the executive's suite of offices, one passes through a long hallway lined with the larger-than-life portraits, in muted colors, of her predecessors, who were all White and male. Upon entering the foyer that leads into the executive's suite of offices, there is an explosion of color. Covering one wall is the pictorial model of the organization's mission statement, depicted as a large, playful mural in bright red, yellow, white, and blue. On the opposite wall there are large, contemporary photographs of the executive at work sites around the country, with children in laboratories, and with prominent business and world leaders. The bulletproof doors and armed guard that served past executives were ordered removed by this executive. Clearly, the executive promoted an open style of communication with the members of her organization. More fundamental however, is the way in which this openness is constructed symbolically through the executive's direct emphasis on her presence as a Black woman among her White predecessors.

Interviews with two of the executive's staff members confirmed this description of her tendency toward openness and the impact on the organization. One staff member said that a major outcome of the executive's efforts is that the amount of communication within the organization has increased since the executive has been in charge. The other staff member reasoned that organizational members had the opportunity to be much clearer about how they contribute to the organization's goals.

In another example of bringing important issues into the open, an executive's supervisor extolled the value of her ability to promote openness at the interpersonal level:

> I think she really practices what she preaches in that area [of] being open with employees] very much. She is, of course, very, very honest with her management, her employees; she doesn't try to manipulate people or try to take a situation that's difficult and make it sound better than what it is. She went through a reorganization here very recently where she did some outsourcing of a lot of employees. And it was handled, I think, as well as any we've done in the company, because she was just very up-front and at the very beginning told everybody what the problems were and what solutions we were looking at, which included potentially outsourcing. And she was very sensitive to their ... to the employees' needs.

Another subtheme related to openness is making sure voices that need to be heard get that opportunity. The primary practice here is making sure that status differences do not thwart efforts to invite organizational participation by all levels of employees. The executives used a number of tactics to reach employees, including interacting directly and in meaningful ways with employees in positions at lower levels of the organization. For instance, one executive reported:

Someone in [one of the field offices] told me that by the time a letter is sent to me, got to me and gone through all of these bureaus, they couldn't even identify the note that they sent. So, as the director, I don't call the people below me to answer questions; I call the folks where I want to talk with them and talk with them directly about whatever the issues are. I spend a lot of time going out to the local field units, doing speaking engagements and talking with them and answering questions for them.

Other tactics to ensure all employees' voices had the potential to be heard include convincing employees that their jobs are directly tied to the organization's effectiveness, "going to bat" across departmental and hierarchical boundaries to secure employees' and departmental interests, and recognizing employees for their work. Employee recognition seemed to be particularly salient among the 15 executives. In the following example, one executive explains how acknowledging employees' efforts is central to motivation, thereby inviting organizational participation:

I show appreciation for what they've done.... And, it's not money; it's not giving them more money, even though we have a responsibility to pay people for what they do. I think the motivation comes from within. It's making people feel good about the type of service they're providing and what they're doing and to show that you truly appreciate what they do, all levels. And that is the challenge I think we have with the corporation.... That's one [practice] I see that we need to spend a lot of time doing. [Since] coming over here the last several months ... [S]ome people have told me—I mean not some, *lots* of people have said, "You know, as long as I've worked here I've never had anybody to tell me that they appreciate what I do. I feel appreciated because I feel like I can see my results but no one has taken the time to say that." And they have just thanked me for recognizing what they've done.

The final subtheme related to openness in communication is having no hidden agendas. The most common expression of this theme was in the staff members' and supervisors' observations that they are always sure where the executive stands. In one instance, an organizational newcomer commented: "I really wasn't expecting it to be like this. But she's a very dynamic person. She's always straightforward. I think most of the time, and by most of the time, I mean 99% of the time, I come out of a meeting knowing where things are, and what her objectives are and her goals, and that sort of thing."

Another executive's supervisor provided a similar description of what it means to have no hidden agendas in communicating leadership:

[I am impressed with] the ability she has to take a problem and get the issue on the table, in other words, you don't sit there trying to listen to a statement and wonder, "What's she really saying?" ... She doesn't make people mad or anything about doing it; she is very good as far as getting the issues [on the table] and let's get 'em resolved and get on to the next thing.

In sum, the openness in communication theme reveals a form of communicating that emphasizes inclusion (i.e., issues, voices) and trust (i.e., no hidden agendas), as important outcomes. What is interesting, however, is how the executives achieve these outcomes through proactively seeking to animate the multiple voices in the leadership context. The process of engaging multiple voices is central to employee empowerment and to the participative decision making practices that inform the fourth leadership theme.

PARTICIPATIVE DECISION MAKING THROUGH COLLABORATIVE DEBATE, AUTONOMY, AND INFORMATION GATHERING

In organizational contexts, a key site for empowerment is decision making, in which empowerment is a process of increased employee participation. Broadly defined, employee participation is "joint decision making with managers on work activities and other aspects of organizational functioning, traditionally considered to be the responsibility or prerogative of management (Seibold & Shea, 2001, p. 666). However, research shows that the ideal of inviting and sustaining employee participation in decision making is often quite different from the reality of the ironies, contradictions, and paradoxes that permeate organizational life (Stohl & Cheney, 2001). For example, Stohl and Cheney's notions of the paradox of agency and the paradox of power add complexity to strategies for employee empowerment. For example, the paradox of agency concerns the individual's sense of efficacy within the system, expressed as "do things our way but in a way that is still distinctively your own" (p. 360). Related to power is the paradox of homogeneity, where organizational leaders may fail to see the value of oppositional voices, excessively valuing agreement, while preaching diversity of opinion.

Paradoxes of participation, such as those related to agency and power, can highlight the tension between structure and creativity. What is important in encountering paradoxes of participation, and what the women's leadership approach reveals, is a process that enables both structure and creativity in a negotiated context. In this study, employee participation was revealed in terms of the more inclusive notion of *employee involvement*, a participative process to engage the entire capacity of workers (Cotton, 1993), enacted through collaborative debate, autonomy, and information gathering.

One tactic the executives use that works through the paradox of homogeneity is a *collaborative debate* structure. As mentioned, the term *collaborative debate* refers to the process of dialectic inquiry in which employees "who are likely to disagree with prevailing opinions are invited to give input" via one-to-one argument and explicit agreement and refutation (Cotton, 1993; Kennedy, 1980, p. 66) for the purpose of collaboratively reaching decisions. One executive, who described the kind of decision making on important issues she does not value, shows a clear example of the collaborative debate tactic in this passage:

> I don't want a serial debate on this issue, where the people who are a little pro come to see me, the people who are a little con come to see me. I would like to debate with everyone in the room. I really do want everybody at the table with varying points of view in this intellectual and technical debate with the yea-sayers and the nay-sayers. Let's hear this debate. But, where this boils down when we talk to real people, is in language so they can understand this. So, let's have this debate in clear, concise language, because we're going to have it with the American public. And that presumes, first of all, to come with a brand new and a very fresh point of view.

In addition to bringing together diverse or conflicting groups, participative decision making also was revealed in descriptions, such as the following, of an executive simply pulling together the groups necessary to move forward on a project that had been stifled by indecision and disagreement. A staff member explained:

> What happens sometimes, is that it becomes difficult to get people to agree around the state, so they drop it. [The executive] is like, "I don't accept status quo, we need to move this for the business, and who is it we need to call or whatever and get this going." And [the executive] got involved and said, "Well why was it dropped?" You know, "We need to pick this back up, because I think it is the right think to do for the business." And she's started to move it, meaning getting in touch with the right people. She has held meetings with the [various groups from around the state] and stepped up to that, where it was kind of just dropped.

Decision autonomy is another decision participation tactic revealed in the data. Employee accounts showed evidence that the executives encouraged departments to be autonomous in making decisions, for example, bringing the executive "in the loop," as one employee phrased it, only when they needed to:

> Today on the conference call, from 3 to 4 we will review [a proposed performance plan] and we will discuss what we feel are the right things. Then, we'll put it in place. Now probably, at some point, we'll bring [the executive] into the loop. But,

[until we make a decision, the executive] says "Here's your revenue, here's your cost, and here's what you need to look like. How you measure the people to get that, that's your call."

In another example of decision autonomy, an executive described how she was restructuring her organization to increase localized decision making:

> I think empowering people means trusting them and pushing the control of the organization as low as we can. How in God's creation can I tell this person what to do at the local county, when their finger is on the pulse of things, not mine? I think I look at it from the bottom-up approach not from a top-down approach.

A final example of decision autonomy more directly captures the paradox of agency. In the following account, an executive in the insurance industry revealed a leadership dilemma she experienced earlier in her career, in which she was charged with helping a division decrease a severe backlog of claims.

> I was asked to take a job and there were maybe two or three managers that had moved to that position prior to that. And if I can remember correctly, one person moved in and he didn't last very long at all.... The job was not just a piece of cake. There were a lot of backlogs, there was a lot of pressure as it related to dealing with providers—they wanted their money. We had... we couldn't get the claims paid very fast. So, it wasn't a job that was easy. In addition to that, and I learned it the very first week on the job, that we were about to lose our government contract because this operation had gotten so bad and we were not as responsive to the customers as we should have been. So, that's very, very major. But if you go into an operation that's strictly manual, paper and you have no type of automation—it just wasn't an easy job. And, I think that's one reason why people didn't necessarily want to stay.... So, I was the third opportunity to get some, to get some stability within that division. And, remember, we were a small company at the time, but he pulled in people from other areas. And, I guess what gave me the confidence that I needed up front was, we had all this help, but yet, some of the same people who were being pulled in to help were more or less compounding the problem because they were, more or less talking to providers and saying oh it's a mess, but let me see what I can do. And, it didn't take long for me to see that the staff in that area needed to be the one to actually pull this, pull us out of the situation we were in, not people from all over the company. I mean, even though we needed the team effort, but we needed the people assigned to that division to take a little bit more ownership of the problem and work together to get it resolved. Once I realized what was happening I did go to [the CEO] and I said to him up front, "you know, you have put me in this position. Either you, you trust me to manage it or you don't ... and he was very supportive and he said "effective in the morning I'm going to pull everybody else out." And that's what he did. So, it was risky but the key to that was ... I pulled the staff together and I did, did say to them that we're, you know, this is something that we're having to deal with, I'm going to need your sup-

port, we're going to need to work overtime. At the time we were not, were not getting the cooperation of the staff because some just refused to work the overtime. And, what we ended up doing was saying, okay, don't necessarily come and say, work every Saturday, because I know you have families, but if you can take work home and work ... what we need everybody to do is put in "x" amount of hours to get us out of this situation. We got 100% cooperation from everybody.

The executive's telling of this narrative reveals the process of embracing both structure—it was clear to everyone that overtime was needed to tackle the backlog—and creativity—she challenged the staff to make their own decisions about how the overtime was to be enacted. What is interesting is that the staff had not bought into the idea of overtime at the requests of the previous managers. The difference seemed to be acknowledging the tensions and conflicts produced by the situation—how is it possible to solve the work problem and maintain some agency?

The third tactic for inviting participation is information gathering as a mechanism for a kind of dispersed listening. Several staff members talked about expecting their opinions to be heard on issues, although on some issues the executive would ultimately make her own decision. One staff member observed:

[The executive] really pays attention to the people who are in the trenches. She gives everybody an opportunity to speak [her or his] piece. And I think she gathers all that information. She utilizes people that are around her to their utmost, because, you know, I think there's strength in what she does, in the way that she does that, it adds to the outcome.

A staff member working in the nonprofit sector emphasized that knowing that she was involved in decision-making was an important motivator to remain with the organization: "I always feel like my advice is going to be taken. It may not always be agreed with, but she is going to listen. That's the biggest motivator right now is that the work is really, if not financially rewarding like the private sector, at least it's recognized."

Collectively, the executives' approaches to decision making revealed a reluctance to accept the status quo. However, there was no evidence that this tendency to challenge the status quo was grounded in a need for competition. Rather the data revealed that these women saw themselves as a conduit through which the diversity of viewpoints could be brought together, negotiated, and enacted.

LEADERSHIP THROUGH BOUNDARY SPANNING

The women's leadership approach reveals a way to negotiate the multiple and complex processes that construct and deconstruct boundaries emerging in 21st-century organizing. The focus is on leadership communication that revisions fixed notions of organizational boundaries characterizing much of the literature on boundary spanning (Finet, 2001). For example prominent views in the strategy literature characterize organizational environments as objective, perceived, and interpreted, presuming real, material environments whose boundaries are clearly distinct from the concrete material organizations located within them. From these more traditional views, boundary-spanning leadership communication is aimed at adapting to, coaligning with, or controlling environmental components and stakeholders, or at processing information scanned from the environment. However, the approach to boundary spanning in the executives' leadership communication reveals an enactment perspective, which implies that "an environment of which strategists can make sense has been put there by strategists' patterns of action—not by a process of perceiving the environment, but by a process of making the environment" (Smircich & Stubbart, 1985, p. 727). This view reveals an understanding of boundaries as permeable and fluid and involving complex enactments of conversation and community building.

The African American women executives in this study demonstrated a mastery of boundary spanning communication as enactment and community building. Their supervisors emphasized how effective the executives are in articulating the organization's mission and purpose to important constituents. One example is from an executive who is superintendent of a large urban school district. Her supervisor, the superintendent to whom she had previously reported in her position as assistant superintendent of curriculum development in another state, described the critical role the executive played in embodying the district's vision for change and creating an environment to support that vision:

> When we brought to the board the need for a major curriculum re-direction that meant that we almost had to take the "road show" out to the people. And [the executive] and I brought that in a number of public forums that we had this year and we did it in a number of presentations to civic and other groups, sometimes together, sometimes separately. As we go into those forums, I'm proud knowing what community reaction to her is going to be. It's always very, very favorable because it is quite evident that she translates this kind of self-assuredness. And where we're going is interpreted by the people out there that the district's in good hands.

The executives themselves view boundary spanning as an opportunity to redefine a community based on a pressing need. This view reinforces an enactment approach that revisions traditional notions of internal and external organizational environments as more fluid configurations of communities of change agents. Not hampered by fixed notions of divisions in functional unit, the executives are active at establishing connections with organizational members with diverse interests, capacities, and responsibilities. "The key to that though has been, not just having the support from the staff that worked directly with me but also, having the support from other divisions and other areas ... It's keeping good rapport with people. I don't know of an area within the company that I don't get good support from."

Finally, many of the women said their positions afforded them opportunities that are specific to them as African American women in majority culture organizations. This included being able to connect in positive ways with the African American community, including those who work for the organization and those who do not. As the following passage reveals, this connection is sometimes a deeply spiritual one that affirms the collective struggle in the African American experience:

> I have come to the Los Angeles area where we have a huge population of African American employees who have not had the opportunity to see people like me and have access to people like me. And it has been just ... they have literally made me cry ... I mean, tears of joy. Just the emotion around ... they are just so genuinely happy to know that there's somebody like me that they can get to know and that I will take time and spend time with them ... I will tell you that, when I first came to LA, I tried to get around to every one of the offices that I lead and we'd shut the office down and I would have like thirty or forty-five minutes talking to the whole crowd. Well one of my offices is here in Los Angeles, and it is predominately African American employees.... The guy who runs the office, he sort of addressed there for about ten or fifteen minutes, and then he handed the mike to me. And I could tell by the looks on their faces ... obviously they don't know me. I have no credibility with these people. Right now, I may be Black but I'm just another senior person dropping by and that they probably won't see again. And so, I took the podium, and I said, "Good morning." And these are fairly young people, you know. They range from probably like twenty-five to early forties kind of thing. But most of them were late twenties early thirties. I said, "Good morning." And I couldn't get eye contact. As I scanned the room, people kind of [mumbled]. "We'd rather be somewhere else. Why are you here?" And then I just stopped and I said ... I stepped away from the podium and I said, "I'm in HOUSE" [waving an arm above her head] like that. And they said, "Woo, I know she's ..." [laughter].

> But you know, you gotta know what to do. Now ... I said that and then I stepped back to that podium and I was all about what we've got to get done for this business and who I am and what I stand for. And, you know what, I had them ... I mean ... they just did not expect that, you know. So, after that, oh, they were lining up to shake my hand and to meet me.

> Several weeks later, I was in that office again and a woman said to me, she said, "Before you leave today, I'd like to talk to you for just a minute." And my first thought was, "Now here's a problem that she thinks I'm going to solve," because employees will do that, you know. They take it all the way somewhere, and they've

never even touched the levels that could really make a difference for them. But I was determined to get to speak to her that day.

And so, I did get a chance [in the cafeteria], and I said, "I know you're having lunch, but I tried to come to your position and you were on the phone ..." and said, "Is this a good time?" And she said, "Oh yes. It will only take a couple of minutes." And she pulled me to the side and she said, "You know," she said, "when you addressed us a few weeks back," she says, "there have been a lot of us ... we have never forgotten that and we have been talking about it, and we want you to know that we see your light shining. And we know that God sent you here." And she said, "The reason why we know that is that when you ..."

(I had a question and answer period after, and you know people were asking me questions, and I always know that a lot of times it's not so much the question, it's like what's behind that question.... And there's not many questions that I ain't heard before. And I really know what they really want to know. And you know, I need to be real clear about, you know, certain things.)

And so she says, "When you were answering those questions," she said, "the reason we know that God sent you here is 'cause you weren't only getting the person who asked the question but you were knocking down sixty more who didn't stand up. And the only way that you could have answered those questions that way was through His help and His guidance."

And, you know I'm telling you ... child, I was ready to start crying in that little lunch room because I didn't stand there and try to profess my religion, I didn't say anything about it, you know. But she said, "We see it." and she said, "We want you to know that we will be praying for you and we just want you to know that you have taken LA by storm, and we just want you to be successful and we've got your back" [e.g. we're behind you].

Other executives said their positions afforded them the opportunity to serve the African American community outside the organization. Several of the women serve on boards that directly address issues facing the African American community. Indeed, my initial contact with two of the women I interviewed for this study was facilitated by their community work.

In summary, the leadership communication themes represent one current interpretation of leadership practices grounded in the experiences of African American women executives within dominant culture organizations. The themes reveal the commonality in the executives' leadership communication, depicting a proactive approach to leadership. More importantly, this approach presents a re-envisioning of leadership based on traditions of resistance and empowerment from African American women's history. In the final chapter, I discuss how these themes and the analytical perspective developed earlier in this paper contributes to the ongoing project of leadership theory building in the twenty-first century.

7

Organizational Leadership Communication in the Twenty-First Century: Toward Inclusive Leadership Theory, Research, and Practice

In this concluding chapter, I discuss the implications of this book for studying leadership communication in postindustrial organizations. The discussion centers on the initial question posed in the Introduction: Whom should we study to learn about leadership? Using this question as an underlying theme, I discuss the implications for seeking diverse sources of leadership knowledge as a way of re-envisioning leadership 21st-century organizations.

SEEKING DIVERSE SOURCES OF LEADERSHIP KNOWLEDGE

The primary implication of this study for leadership theorizing is that we should continue to seek diverse sources of knowledge. In the past, organizational leadership research has been implicitly guided by the question, What can we learn about leadership from the perspective of assumed White privilege? What I have demonstrated in this research is that it is fruitful to learn about organizational leadership from the perspectives of people who struggle against race, gender, and class oppression. There are several important contributions of this study of

African American women executives that affirm the value of seeking diverse sources of leadership knowledge.

Recognizing the Centrality of Race and Difference in Organizing

One implication of this study is that centering previously muted and marginalized voices illuminates underlying processes of domination, exclusion, and containment in leadership theory development and organizational practice. As pointed out in this volume, organizations emphasize monoculturalism in the workplace, even as they advocate multicultural and diversity programs. This emphasis on monoculturalism presumes an absence of racial, gender, and class conflict (Prasad et al., 1997). Yet the fragmented and disconnected communicative contexts of postindustrial organization presuppose the existence and even increase in such conflict (Cheney et al., 2004). Thus, it is important to disrupt the focus on race- and gender-neutral theory development.

As demonstrated in this volume, one way of achieving this is to begin with inclusive theoretical frameworks that differently attend to multiple systems of oppression such as race, class, and gender. In this volume, I draw upon the work of Nkomo, (1992) and others (Acker, 1991; Ashcraft, in press; Calàs & Smircich, 1996; Collins, 1998a, 1998b; Parker, 2003; also see Allen, in press) who provide exemplars of frameworks for studying difference in organizations. Each of these frameworks emphasizes the need to focus on marginalized voices that have been excluded from previous frameworks.

Another way of achieving this focus on race and difference in organizing is to produce more studies of how race and difference are constituted in organizing and leadership processes. This study provides some preliminary insight. For example, the women perceived that the interactions in which race and gender difference seemed most salient were with White male peers and African American co-workers. One interpretation of this finding is that the power relationships among co-workers are not well-defined in the formal organizational structure, as are the superior–subordinate relationships. Therefore, it may be more likely that the sites of negotiating power and identity issues in complex organizations in general would occur at the co-worker interaction level as organizational members work out the terms of their participation (Stohl & Cheney, 2000). At the same time, it would be interesting to learn more about how this dynamic changes in the leadership context as race and gender difference becomes redefined in the postindustrial age.

Reclaiming Cultural Traditions

Another important contribution of this book is that it provides an opportunity to reclaim a cultural tradition that for too long has gone unacknowledged and devalued. For African American women, this reclaiming represents a counter narrative to combat the forces that stigmatize and demonize Black women (Dyson, 2003). By illuminating and deconstructing the cultural texts that have devalued African American women's contributions to leadership knowledge, this study serves to challenge controlling images of women as leaders, opening up the possibility for more flexible understandings of gender and leadership. Rather than reproducing the hierarchical viewpoints that have dominated leadership theorizing, it is more revealing to study groups in their own right and to see the relationship of all groups to the structure of race, class, and gender relations through society (Andersen & Collins, 1992).

When viewed as cultural tradition, African American women's history of survival, resistance and change can be seen as leadership knowledge communicated from generation to generation. This idea is not unlike that which underlies traditional theories of leadership and nepotism in business (Bellow, 2003). European-American cultural narratives emphasize leadership traditions being passed down father to son. The rites of passage that ensure some middle- and upper-class White men privileged positions of leadership at the top of America's corporations and institutions are socially constructed as the standard for success in the traditional leadership literature (cf., Kotter, 1982; Mintzberg, 1973). The experiences and knowledge that have, as Hine and Thompson (1998) noted, "enabled Black women to shape the raw materials of their lives into an extraordinary succession of victories" (p. 5) have been ignored and unexamined.

This book serves to center African American women's tradition of leadership. Other untapped sources of leadership knowledge should be uncovered and incorporated into the study of organizational leadership. "Best Practices" derived from other cultural experiences related to, for example age, class, ethnicity, and so on, can be incorporated into a complex, rich, understanding of leadership for 21st-century organizing (e.g., see Bennis & Thomas, 2002).

Continuing Cultural Traditions in Postindustrial Society

A third contribution emerging from this study is that situating the leadership approaches of contemporary African American women into historical perspective confirms the organic character of leadership knowledge production and, at the same time, points to the challenges of continuing traditions of leadership in a social world that is increasingly revealed as fragmented and disconnected.

When viewed as a cultural tradition, Black women's history of survival, resistance and change can be seen as leadership knowledge communicated from generation to generation. However, current shifts in the economic and social structuring, of society presents new challenges in continuing the cultural tradition of resistance and transformation that marked African American women's history. For example, current conditions and discourses seem to emphasize class barriers in a way that has not been so demonstrated in the past.

In the current economy, African American girls and young women in working-class and poor socioeconomic contexts are among the most vulnerable populations (Browne, 1999). Yet the empowerment of African American adolescent girls is often neglected in social policy initiatives that focus on African American youth. However there is clearly a need to focus on this group. For contemporary African American girls across socioeconomic statuses, the potential for success occurs within a complex social, cultural, and political environment that, by many important measures, is becoming increasingly difficult for them to navigate (Holcomb-McCoy & Moore-Thomas, 2001; Twine, 2000). African American adolescent girls, particularly those living in impoverished neighborhoods with high crime rates, are at risk for low academic achievement, teen pregnancy, drug abuse, and becoming victims of violence (Arnold, 1994).

Moreover, they are contending with racialized images in the press and popular media of African American women as Welfare Queens, and Video Divas, juxtaposed with inaccessible images of the Overachieving Black Lady and the Ideal White Woman (Collins, 1998a; Fordham, 1993; Lubiano, 1992; Radford-Hill, 2002). At the same time, patterns of deindustrialization, declining labor markets, and continued residential segregation by race, contribute to the fragmented social world for contemporary African American girls and young women, as well as other groups such as Latinas and Native American girls and women (Browne, 1999). However, in hopeful contrast, there are signs that, in the tradition of their foremothers, young African American women and teenage girls are seeking to remain self-defined and express a range of identities as Black women in a complex cultural milieu (Chambers, 2003; Fordham 1993; Springer, 1999).

Foregrounding Diverse Cultural Leadership Traditions

A final contribution of this research for seeking diverse sources of knowledge is that it demonstrates the importance of placing marginalized groups at the center of analysis to disrupt the silences that devalue their contributions to knowledge production. By placing African American women at the center of a study of organizational leadership, this research serves an emancipative function, giving voice to a tradition of knowledge and communication practices grounded in Black women's experiences. In asking the women in this study to speak for themselves—to be self-defining—this research helps to shatter the controlling images of Black women that are created through racist and sexist ideologies (Christian, 1980; Lubiano, 1992; Morton, 1991; Walker, 1983).

This study adds to the growing body of research that looks at traditionally marginalized persons from their own viewpoints, giving voice to previously muted cultural traditions (Allen, 1996, 1998, 2000; Gonzalez, Houston, & Chen, 1997; Hecht, Ribeau, & Roberts, 1989; Orbe, 1998; Shuter & Turner, 1997).

In addition, this research serves as a basis for promoting cross cultural interaction within contemporary organizations. Marlene Fine (1995) defined cultural sensitivity in terms of three components, with each building developmentally on the previous component: (1) recognition of cultural differences, (2) knowledge about cultural differences, and (3) suspension of judgment about cultural differences. This study provides important cultural information—grounded qualitative descriptions of African American women executives' communication—that might benefit persons who work with African American women executives, encouraging them to reject their preconceived images of Black women that may be based on stereotyping. Fine (1995) argued that developing *multicultural literacy*—which emerges from an attitude of cultural sensitivity—is essential for survival in a multicultural society. Similarly, Shuter and Turner (1997) pointed out, "With diversity growing in corporate America, it is important that culturally driven stylistic differences are understood and appreciated by managers and employees" (p. 92). Hopefully, this research will contribute to increased multicultural understanding.

CONCLUSION

One of the greatest challenges in postindustrial organizing is creating communicative environments in which people find meaning and connection in a social world that is increasingly fragmented and disconnected. In this book I used a critical feminist perspective to examine African American women executives' leadership communication within majority White, male-dominated organizations in the United States. By placing African American women at the center of analysis, this research challenged the hegemonic discourses that limit African American women's access to the meaning-making process in leadership theory. As a result, this study revealed new ways of thinking about instrumental and collaborative leadership.

In the twenty-first century, leadership theorizing should reflect the interplay and struggle of the multiple discourses that characterize postindustrial society.

An important role of leadership is most certainly to animate (i.e., bring to the foreground) and then facilitate the negotiation of this interplay. In the present study, this process is revealed in an interactive approach to leadership in which the executives see themselves as a conduit through which a diversity of viewpoints could be brought together, negotiated, and enacted. We should continue to explicate theories of leadership that acknowledge the facilitation of multivocality as a central process.

The themes that summarize African American women's traditions of leadership as an exemplar of best leadership practices are not intended as a final vocabulary on African American women's approaches to leadership and organizing. Rather they are put forth as a beginning—a positioning of cultural experience into the center of the study of organizational leadership. For too long, African American women's strength as leaders has gone unacknowledged, devalued, and otherwise marginalized. My hope is that future studies of African American women leaders will broaden and enrich the leadership themes presented in this volume.

Appendix A:
Interview Protocols

Leader Interview Protocol

Overview

I. The interview will focus on organizational leadership from your perspective as an African American women executive in a majority White U.S. organization.

II. The interview will last about 1 hour and will cover three major areas:
1. The childhood, adolescent, and professional experiences that most influenced your current leadership approach.
2. Barriers and opportunities for your leadership effectiveness in Majority White organizations.
3. Your current leadership approach.

PART I:

Let's start by discussing the life experiences that most influenced your leadership development beginning with your early childhood.
1. First, tell me about *your family*.
   a. What was the size and composition of your family?
   —Where were you in the birth order?
   b. Tell me about your mother and father (or other person(s) that reared you).

—What were their roles within your family?

—What were/are their occupations?

—What was/is their educational background?

c. Are there any parental behaviors or attitudes that you admired as a child and that you have come to reflect or emulate as an adult? Please describe them.

d. What were some of the important messages that you received from your parents that you feel helped to shape who you are today?

2. What *other adults*, other than your parents, influenced you during your childhood and early adolescence?

a. behaviors or attitudes that you have come to reflect or emulate?

b. important messages that you feel helped to shape who you are today?

3. Focusing on the *high school and college years*, describe any critical incidents, significant experiences, persons, or events that influenced your leadership development.

a. What did you learn about leadership from these influences?

b. When did you recognize yourself as a leader?

4. Now, let's discuss your *career track*

a. What specific obstacles did you have to overcome/deal with as you progressed through your career?

b. What instances of discrimination (differential treatment) have you encountered as you progressed in your career?

1. What happened? Where did it occur? Who was involved?

2. Why do you think this incident occurred?

3. What was your response?

4. In retrospect, how would you have handled the incident differently, if at all?

c. What lessons did you learn as a result of your experiences as you progressed through your career?

1. What would you do differently?

5. As you reflect on your life experiences, what do you consider the most significant influences on your development as a leader?

PART II

Let us now discuss the barriers and opportunities for your leadership effectiveness in this organization.

1. Of all the accomplishments you have made during your tenure as part of senior management, of what accomplishment are you most proud? Why?

a. Tell me about one of the most difficult situations you've faced as the (state position in senior management).

2. In what ways does being [one of] the only African American women at the senior level affect you and the way you do your job?

   a. Do you think people respond differently to you as an African American woman than they would, say, a White woman in the same position?

      1. Why or why not?

      2. If so, in what way is the response different? What is an example of when this occurred?

      3. If so, how did you adjust your behavior, if at all?

3. Describe your interactions with the other members of senior management.

   a. In what contexts (work/nonwork) do you interact with other senior managers?

   b. How often do you interact with other senior managers? What is usually discussed (work or nonwork-related topics?)

   c. How accepted do you feel as a part of senior management? Explain.

4. Why do you think there are so few African American women managers at the senior level in this company?

   a. What advice would you give an African American woman manager who is aspiring to move into senior management? Why that advice?

PART III

Now let us talk more specifically about your leadership behavior and communication.

1. What is your [stated] goal or mission for your [unit]?

   a. Why this goal statement?

   b. By what means do you communicate your goals and mission for your [unit]?

2. Describe your philosophy of leadership (in other words, what do you feel is the best way to get people to follow your leadership?)

   a. Give me an example of something you've done that you think clearly demonstrates your leadership approach (e.g., a specific project or idea you implemented).

   b. Tell me about a time when you have felt resistance from your staff, peers, superiors, or clients. How did you handle such resistance?

3. In what ways does your leadership philosophy compare to what you have observed in the way others exercise leadership in this organization?

   a. Compare your leadership approach to that of your predecessor's.

4. Let's talk about how you use communication in your daily routine
   a. As you carry out your responsibilities, with whom do you spend the most time in interaction? (Staff? Peers? Board? External constituents?) Why?
   b. How many formal meetings do you hold per month?
      —Describe a typical meeting
   c. What is your primary means for getting information in this organization?
      —source?
      —What mechanism (face to face, telephone, etc.)
      —Any obstacles?
5. What specific behaviors and communication strategies do you use to influence others in this organization?
   a. What strategies do you use to encourage high performance among employees?
   b. How do you handle poor performers?
   c. What methods of rewarding employees seem to work best?
6. Describe your approach to conflict management.
   a. With whom do you experience the most conflict in your organizational interactions? White males? White females? Black males? Black females?

To conclude the interview, what are at least three ground rules you think every African American woman should follow in order to be a successful organizational leader?

1. What else would you add about your experiences as a leader in this organization that we have not discussed?
2. Thank you for your participation in this study.
3. May I contact you if necessary to clarify/augment answers?
4. Summary of the results will be made available. May I forward a copy to you?

Follower Interview Protocol

Overview

1. The interview will focus on the follower's descriptions of the executive's leadership approach and how the leader has impacted the organization.
2. The interview will last about 30 minutes and will be taped.

Questions for Follower

1. Tell me about your history with _____.
   a. When did you first meet?
   b. How long have you worked together?
2. Tell me about the kind of leader _____ is.
   a. How would you describe your interaction with her?
   —What is an example that demonstrates this?
   b. What is her communication style?
   c. How are decisions made?
   —How much input do you have in making decisions?
   d. Would you say this leader is more task oriented or people oriented?
   —Why? Give an example to demonstrate your answer.
   —Give me an example that demonstrates these behaviors being rewarded.
   e. How does the leader motivate people in the organization?
   —Describe a typical meeting with this leader.
   —Does she give pep talks? Describe a typical one.
   —How often do you receive memos from the leader?
3. Tell me about the degree of impact this leader has made on the (department/division)?
   a. Describe the leader's vision for the department/division?
   —How does she communicate that vision?
   —If you can, tell me how that vision differs from the visions of previous leaders of this division?
   b. How have things changed during the time _____ has been in charge?
   —How has decision making changed?
   —How have the way things get done changed (e.g., reporting structures, etc.)?
   c. If this leader were to leave this organization today, what three things would most people remember about her leadership in this organization?

Close

1. What else should I know about _____ as a leader?
2. Thank you for your help with my research.

Supervisor Interview Protocol

Overview

1. The interview will focus on the supervisor's descriptions of the executive's leadership approach and how the leader has impacted the organization.
2. The interview will last about 30 minutes and will be taped.

Questions For Supervisor

1. Tell me about your history with _____.
   a. When did you first meet?
   b. How long have you worked together?
2. Tell me about the kind of leader _____ is.
   a. Describe her approach to getting things done.
      —Is she more task oriented or people oriented? Explain.
   b. What is her communication style? What is an example that demonstrates this?
   c. What is her approach to getting your approval on ideas she wants implemented? Give me an example that demonstrates this.
   d. Complete this sentence: "When the pressure is on, the one thing I can count on from _____ is ..."
3. Tell me about the degree of impact this leader has made on her division.
   a. Describe the leader's vision for the division?
      —How does she communicate that vision?
      —If you can, tell me how that vision differs from the visions of previous leaders in this organization?
   b. How have things changed during the time _____ has been in charge?
      —How has decision making changed?
      —How have the way things get done changed (e.g., reporting structures, etc.)?
   c. If this leader were to leave this organization today, what three things would most people remember about her leadership in this organization?

Close

1. What else should I know about _____ as a leader?
2. Thank you for your help with my research.

References

Acker, J. (1991). Hierarchies, jobs, bodies: A theory of gendered organizations. In J. Lorber & S. A. Farrell (Eds.), *The social construction of gender* (pp. 162–179). Newbury Park, CA: Sage.

Allen, B. J. (1995). "Diversity" and organizational communication. *Journal of Applied Communication Research, 23,* 143–155.

Allen, B. J. (1996, Winter). Feminist standpoint theory: A Black woman's (re)view of organizational socialization. *Communication Studies, 47,* 257–271.

Allen, B. J. (1998). Black womanhood and feminist standpoints. *Management Communication Quarterly, 11*(4), 575–586.

Allen, B. J. (2000). "Learning the ropes": A Black feminist standpoint analysis. In P. M. Buzzanell (Ed.), *Rethinking organizational and managerial communication from feminist perspectives* (pp. 177–208). Thousand Oaks, CA: Sage.

Allen, B. J. (2004). *Difference matters: Communicating social identity.* Long Grove, IL: Waveland Press.

Alvesson, M., & Billing, Y. D. (1997). *Understanding gender and organizations.* London: Sage.

Amott, T., & Matthaei, J. (Eds.). (1996). *Race, Gender, and work: A multicultural economic history of women in the United States* (2nd ed.). Boston: South End Press.

Andersen, H. C. (1968). *Forty-two stories.* (M. R. James, Trans.). London: Faber & Faber. (original work published, 1837).

Andersen, M. L., & Collins, P. H. (1992). *Race, class, and gender: An anthology.* Belmont, CA: Wadsworth Publishing Company.

Aptheker, B. (1982). *Woman's legacy: Essays on race, sex, and class in American history.* Amherst: The University of Massachusetts Press.

Arnold, R. (1994). Black women in prison: The price of resistance. In M. Baca Zinn & B. T. Dill (Eds.), *Women of color in U.S. society* (pp. 171–184). Philadelphia: Temple University Press.

Ashcraft, K. (in press). Gender, discourse, and organization: Framing a shifting relationship. In D. Grant, C. Hardy, C. Oswick, N. Phillips, & L. Putnam (Eds.), *The Sage Handbook of Organization Discourse.* Thousand Oaks, CA: Sage.

100

Ashcraft, K. (2000). Empowering "professional" relationships: Organizational communication meets feminist practice. *Management Communication Quarterly 13,* 347–392.

Ashcraft (2001). Organized dissonance: Feminist bureaucracy as hybrid form. *Academy of Management Journal 44,* 1301–1322.

Ashcraft, K., & Allen, B. J. (2003). The racial foundation of organizational communication. *Communication Theory, 31,* 5–38.

Avolio, B., & Bass, B. M. (2002). *Developing potential across a full range of leadership: Cases on transactional and transformational leadership.* Mahwah, NJ: Lawrence Erlbaum Associates.

Barge, J. K. (1994). *Leadership Communication: Skills for organizations and groups.* New York: St. Martin's Press.

Bass, B. M. (1985). *Leadership and performance beyond expectations.* New York: Free Press.

Baxter, L. A., & Montgomery, B. M. (1996). *Relating: Dialogue and dialectics.* New York: Guilford.

Bass, B. M. (1990). *Bass & Stogdill's handbook of leadership: Theory, research, & managerial applications.* New York: Free Press.

Bederman, G. (1995). *Manliness & Civilization: A cultural history of gender and race in the United States, 1880–1917.* Chicago: University of Chicago Press.

Bell, E. L., & Nkomo, S. (1992). *The glass ceiling vs. the concrete wall: Career perceptions of White and African-American women managers* (working paper no. 3470–92). Massachusetts Institute of Technology.

Bell, E. L., & Nkomo, S. (2001). *Our separate ways: Black and White women and the struggle for professional identity.* Boston: Harvard Business School Press.

Bellow, A. (2003). *In praise of nepotism: A natural history.* New York: Doubleday.

Bem, S. (1974). The measurement of psychological androgyny. *Journal of Consulting and Clinical Psychology, 42,* 155–162.

Bennis, W., & Nanus, B. (1985). *The strategies for taking charge.* New York: Harper & Row.

Bennis, W., & Biederman, P. W. (1997). *Organizing genius: The secrets of creative collaboration.* Reading, MA: Addison-Wesley.

Bennis, W. G., & Thomas, R. T. (2002). *Geeks & geezers: How era, values, and defining moments shape leaders.* Boston: Harvard Business School Press.

Bensen, J. K. (1977). Organizations: A dialectical view. *Administrative Science Quarterly, 22,* 1–20.

Berger, P., & Luckmann, T. (1966). *The social construction of reality.* Garden City, NY: Anchor.

Biggart, N. W., & Hamilton, G. G. (1984). The power of obedience. *Administrative Science Quarterly, 29*(4), 540–549.

Blassingame, J. (Ed.). (1979). *New perspectives on Black studies.* Urbana: University of Illinois Press.

Blumer, H. (1969). *Symbolic interactionism: Perspective and method.* Englewood Cliffs, N. J.: Prentice Hall.

Browne, I. (Ed.). (1999). *Latinas and African American women at work: Race, gender, and economic inequality.* New York: Russell Sage Foundation.

Browning, L. D. (1992). Lists and stories as organizational communication. *Communication Theory, 2,* 281–302.

Bruner, J. (1990). *Acts of meaning.* Cambridge, MA: Harvard University Press.

Buckley, K. W., & Steffy, J. (1986). The invisible side of leadership. In J. A. Adams (Ed.), *Transforming leadership* (pp. 233–243). Alexandria, VA: Miles River Press.

Bullis, C. (1993). At least it's a start. In S. Deetz (Ed.), *Communication Yearbook 16* (pp. 144–154). Newbury Park, CA: Sage.

Burgess, N., & Horton, H. D. (1993). African American women and work: A socio-historical perspective. *Journal of Family History, 18*(1) 53–63.

Burns, J. M. (1978). *Leadership*. New York: Harper and Row.

Buzzanell, P. M. (1994). Gaining a voice: Feminist perspectives in organizational communication. *Management Communication Quarterly, 7,* 339–383.

Buzzanell, P. M. (Ed.). (2000). *Rethinking organizational and managerial communication from feminist perspectives.* Thousand Oaks, CA: Sage.

Buzzanell, P., Ellingson, L., Silvio, C., Pasch, V., Dale, B., Mauro, G., Smith, E., Weir, N., & Martin, C. (2002). Leadership processes in alternative organizations: Invitational and dramaturgical leadership. *Communication Studies, 48,* 285–310.

Calàs, M. (1987). *Organization science/fiction: The postmodern in the management disciplines.* Unpublished doctoral dissertation, Amherst: University of Massachusetts.

Calàs, M. (1993). Deconstructing charismatic leadership: Re-reading Weber from the darker side. *Leadership Quarterly, 4,* 305–328.

Calàs, M. B., & Smircich, L. (1988). Reading leadership as a form of cultural analysis. In J. G. Hunt, B. R. Baliga, H. P. Dachler, & C. A. Schriescheim (Eds.), *Emerging leadership vistas* (pp. 201–226). Lexington, MA: Lexington Books.

Calàs, M. B., & Smircich, L. (1993, March/April). Dangerous liaisons: The "feminine-in-management" meets "globalization." *Business Horizons,* 71–81.

Calàs, M. B., & Smircich, L. (1996). From the "Woman's" point of view: Feminist approaches to organization studies. In S. Clegg, C. Hardy, & W. R. Nord (Eds.), *Handbook of organization studies* (pp. 218–257). London: Sage.

Cavanaugh, J. M. (1997). (In)corporating the Other? Managing the politics of workplace difference. In P. Prasad, A. J. Mills, M. Elmes, & A. Prasad (Eds.), *Managing the organizational melting pot: Dilemmas of workplace diversity* (pp. 31–53). Thousand Oaks, CA: Sage.

Chambers, V. (2003). *Black women and success: Having it all?* New York: Doubleday.

Cheney, G., Christensen, L., Zorn, T., & Ganesh, S. (2004). *Organizational Communication in an Age of Globalization: Issues, Reflections, Practices.* Prospect Height, IL: Waveland Press.

Christian, B. (1980). *Black women novelists: The development of a tradition, 1892–1976.* Westport, CT: Greenwood Press.

Clinton, C. (1982). *The plantation mistress: Woman's world in the Old South.* New York: Pantheon Books.

Collins, P. H. (1986). Learning from the outsider within: The sociological significance of Black feminist thought. *Social Problems, 33*(6), 14–32.

Collins, P H. (1990). *Black feminist thought: Knowledge, consciousness, and the politics of empowerment.* Boston: Unwin Hyman.

Collins, P. H. (1998a). *Fighting words: Black women and the search for justice.* Minneapolis: University of Minnesota Press.

Collins, P. H. (1998b). Toward a new vision: Race, class, and gender as categories of analysis and connection. In M. L. Anderson & P. H. Collins (Eds.), *Race, class, and gender: An anthology* (pp. 213–223). Belmont, CA: Wadsworth.

Collins, P. H. (2002). Symposium on West and Fenstermaker's "Doing Difference." In S. Fenstermaker, & C. West (Eds.), *Doing gender, doing difference: Inequality, power, and institutional change* (pp. 8–84). New York: Routledge.

Conger, J. A. (1989). Inspiring others: The language of leadership. *The Executive, 5,* 31–45.

Connell, R. (1995). *Masculinities.* Cambridge, U.K.: Polity Press.

Cooper, A. J. (1892). *A voice from the South.* Xenia, OH: Aldine Printing House.

Cotton, J. L. (1993). *Employee involvement: Methods for improving performance and work attitudes.* Newbury Park, CA: Sage.

Dansereau, F. (1995a). Leadership: The multiple-level approaches, Part I. *Leadership Quarterly, 6,* 97–247.

Dansereau, F. (1995b). Leadership: The multiple-level approaches, Part 2. *Leadership Quarterly, 6,* 249–450.

Davis, A. Y. (1981). *Women, race, and class.* New York: Random House.

Davis, M. (Ed.). (1982). *Contributions of Black women to America* (Vol. 1). Columbia, SC: Kenday Press.

Deetz, S. A. (1992). *Democracy in an age of corporate colonization.* Albany, NY: SUNY Press.

Deetz, S. A. (1995). *Transforming communication.* Albany, N.Y.: SUNY Press.

Deetz, S. A. (2003). Corporate governance, communication, and getting social values into the decisional chain. *Management Communication Quarterly, 16,* 606–611.

Deetz, S. A., Tracy, S., Simpson, J. L. (2000). *Leading organizations through transitions: Communication and cultural change.* Thousand Oaks, CA: Sage.

Delgado, R. (1995). Introduction. In R. Delgado (Ed.), *Critical race theory: The cutting edge.* Philadelphia: Temple University Press.

Dill, B. T. (1979). *Across the barriers of race and class: An exploration of the relationship between work and family among Black female domestic servants.* Unpublished doctoral dissertation. New York University.

Dougherty, D., & Krone, K. (2000). Overcoming the dichotomy: Cultivating standpoints in organizations through research. *Women's Studies in Communication, 23*(1), 16–40.

Dugger, K. (1991). Social location and gender role attitudes: A comparison of Black and White women. In B. Lorber & S. Farrell (Eds.), *The social construction of gender* (pp. 38–55). Newbury Park, CA: Sage.

Dyson, M. E. (2003). *Why I love Black women.* New York: Basic Civitas Books.

Eagly, A. H. (1987). *Sex differences in social behavior: A social-role interpretation.* Hillsdale, NJ: Lawrence Erlbaum Associates.

Eagly, A. H., & Karau, S. S. (1991). Gender and the emergence of leaders: A meta-analysis. *Journal of Personality and Social Psychology, 60,* 685–710.

Ely, R. (1991). Gender difference: What difference does it make? *Academy of Management best paper proceedings,* 363–367.

Essed, P. (1991). *Understanding everyday racism.* Newbury Park: Sage.

Essed, P. (1994). Contradictory positions, ambivalent perceptions: A case study of a Black woman entrepreneur. In K. Bhavnani & A. Phoenix (Eds.), *Shifting identities, shifting racisms: A feminism & psychology reader* (pp. 99–118). London: Sage.

Etter-Lewis, G. (1993). *My soul is my own: Oral narratives of African American women in the professions.* New York: Routledge.

Fairclough, N. (1992). *Discourse and social change.* Cambridge, U.K.: Polity Press.

Fairclough, N. (1995). *Critical discourse analysis: The Critical study of language.* London: Longman.

Fairhurst, G. T. (2001). Dualisms in leadership research. In F. M. Jablin & L. L. Putnam (Eds.), *The new handbook of organizational communication* (pp. 379–439). Thousand Oaks, CA: Sage.

Fairhurst, G. T., & Saar, R. A. (1996). The art of framing: Managing the language of leadership. San Francisco: Jossey-Bass.

Fine, M. (1995). Building successful multicultural organizations. Westport, CT: Quorum Books.

Fine, M., & Buzzanell, P. (2000). Walking the high wire: Leadership theorizing, daily acts, and tensions. In P. Buzzanell (Ed.), Rethinking organizational and managerial communication from feminist perspectives (pp. 128–156). Thousand Oaks, CA: Sage.

Finet, D. (2001). Sociopolitical environments and issues. In F. M. Jablin & L. L. Putnam (Eds.), The new handbook of organizational communication: Advances in theory, research, and methods (pp. 270–290). Newbury Park, CA: Sage.

Fisher, B. A. (1985). Leadership as medium: Treating complexity in group communication research. Small Group Behavior, 16, 167–196.

Fisher, B. A. (1986). Leadership: When does the difference make a difference? In R. Hirokawa & M. S. Poole (Eds.), Communication and group decision-making (pp. 197–215). Beverly Hills, CA: Sage.

Fletcher, J. (1994). Castrating the female advantage: Feminist standpoint research and management science. Journal of Management Inquiry, 3, 74–82.

Flores, L. A., & Moon, D. G. (2002). Race traitor. Western Journal of Communication, 66, 181–207.

Fondas, N. (1997). Feminization unveiled: Management qualities in contemporary writings. Academy of Management Review, 22, 257–282.

Fordham, S. (1993). "Those loud Black girls": Black women, silence, and gender, "passing" in the academy. Anthropology and Education Quarterly, 24(1), 3–32.

Forman, J. (1985). The making of Black revolutionaries. Washington, DC: Open Hand.

Foster, W. F. (1989). Toward a critical practice of leadership. In J. Smyth (Ed.), Critical perspectives on educational leadership (pp. 39–62). London: Falmer.

Fra-Molinero, B. (1995). The condition of Black women in Spain during the renaissance. In K. M. Vaz (Ed.), Black Women in America (pp. 159–178).Thousand Oaks, CA: Sage.

Garfinkel, H. (1967). Studies in ethnomethodology. Englewood Cliffs, NJ: Prentice Hall.

Gergen, M. (1990). Baskets of reed and arrows of steel: Stories of chaos and continuity. In S. Srivastva (Ed.), Symposium: Executive and organizational continuity. Cleveland, OH: Case Western Reserve University, Weatherhead School of Management, Department of Organizational Behavior.

Giddens, A. (1991). Modernity and self-identity: Self and society in the late modern age. Cambridge, U.K.: Polity Press.

Giddings, P. (1984). When and where I enter: The impact of Black women on race and sex in America. New York: William Morrow.

Gilkes, C. T. (1980). Holding back the ocean with a broom: Black women and community work. In L. Rogers-Rose (Ed.), The Black woman (pp. 217–32). Beverly Hills, CA: Sage.

Gittell, M., Ortega-Bustamante, I., & Steffy, T. (1999). Women creating social capital and social change: A study of women-led community development organizations. New York: Howard Samuels State Management and Policy Center, The Graduate School and University Center, City University of New York.

Goffman, E. (1976). Gender display. Studies in the Anthropology of Visual Communication, 3, 69–77.

Goffman, E. (1977). The arrangement between the sexes. Theory & Society, 4, 301–331.

Gonzalez, A., Houston, M., & Chen, V. (Eds.). (1997). *Our voices: Essays in culture, ethnicity, and communication* (2nd ed.). Los Angeles: Roxbury.

Grant, J. (1998). *Ella Baker: Freedom Bound*. New York: Wiley.

Greenleaf, R. K. (1977). *Servant leadership: A journey into the nature of legitimate power and greatness*. New York: Paulist Press.

Grimes, D. S. (2002). Challenging the status quo? Whiteness in the diversity management literature. *Management Communication Quarterly,15*(3), 381–409.

Grossman, H., & Chester, N. (1990). *The experience and meaning of work in women's lives*. Hillsdale, NJ: Lawrence Erlbaum Associates.

Guinier, L., & Torres, G. (2002). *The miner's canary: Enlisting race, resisting power, transforming democracy*. Cambridge, MA: Harvard University Press.

Gyant, L. (1990). *Contributions of African American women to nonformal education during the Civil Rights Movement, 1955–1966*. Unpublished doctoral dissertation, Pennsylvania State University.

Haraway, D. J. (1997). *Modest witness@second millennium: Femaleman meets Oncomouse*. New York: Routledge.

Harding, S. (1987). Introduction: Is there a feminist method? In S. Harding (Ed.), *Feminism & methodology*. Milton Keynes: Open University Press.

Harding, S. (1991). *Whose science? Whose knowledge? Thinking from women's lives*. Ithaca, NY: Cornell University Press.

Harding, S. (1996). Gendered ways of knowing and the "epistemological crisis" of the West. In N. Goldberger, J. Tarule, B. Clinchy, & M. Belenky (Eds.), *Knowledge, difference, and power: Essays inspired by Women's ways of knowing* (pp. 431–454). New York: Basic Books.

Harley, S. (1997). Speaking up: The politics of Black women's labor history. In E. Higginbotham & M. Romero (Eds.), *Women and work: Exploring race, ethnicity, and class* (pp. 28–51). Thousand Oaks, CA: Sage.

Hartsock, N. (1987). The feminist standpoint: Developing the ground for a specifically feminist historical materialism. In S. Harding (Ed.), *Feminism & methodology* (pp. 157–180). Bloomington: Indiana University Press.

Hartwick Humanities in Management Institute. (2003). *Hartwick classic leadership cases*. Oneonta, NY: Hartwick College.

Hecht, M., Ribeau, S., & Roberts, J. K. (1989). An Afro-American perspective on interethnic communication. *Communication Monographs, 56*(4), 385–410.

Helgesen, S. (1990). *The female advantage: Women's ways of leadership*. New York: Doubleday.

Heifetz, R. A. (1994). *Leadership without easy answers*. Cambridge, MA: Belknap.

Heifetz, R. A., & Laurie, D. L. (1997). The work of leadership. *Harvard Business Review, 75*(1), 124–134.

Henderson, M. G. (1989). Speaking in Tongues: Dialogics, dialects, and the Black woman writer's literary tradition. In C. A. Wall (Ed.), *Changing our own words: Essays on criticism, theory, and writing by Black women*. New Brunswick, NJ: Rutgers University Press.

Henri, F. (1975). *Black migration: Movement North, 1900–1920, the road from myth to man*. New York: Anchor Press.

Hine, D. C. (Ed.). (1993). *Black women in America* (Vols. 1–2). Brooklin, NY: Carlson.

Hine, D. C., & Thompson, K. (1998). *A shining thread of hope: The history of Black women in America*. New York: Broadway Books.

Hirschmann, N. J. (1997). Feminist standpoint as postmodern strategy. In S. J. Kenney & H. Kinsella (Eds.), *Politics and feminist standpoint theories* (pp. 73–92). New York: Haworth.

Holcomb-McCoy, C. C., & Moore-Thomas, C. (2001, October). Empowering African-American adolescent females. *Professional School Counseling, 5,* 19–27.

hooks, b. (1981). *Ain't I a woman: Black women and feminism.* Boston: South End Press.

hooks, b. (1984). *Feminist theory from margin to center.* Boston: South End Press.

hooks, b. (1990). *Yearning: Race, gender, and cultural politics.* Boston: South End.

Horne, G. (2000). *Race woman: The lives of Shirley Graham Du Bois.* New York: New York University Press.

Hull, G. T., Scott, P. B., & Smith, B. (Eds.). (1982). *All the women are White, all the men are Black, but some of us are brave: Black women's studies.* Old Westbury, NY: Feminist Press.

Isaacs, W. N. (1993). Taking flight: Dialogue, collective thinking, and organizational learning. *Organizational Dynamics, 22,* 24–39.

Isaacs, W. N. (1999). *Dialogue: The art of thinking together.* New York: Currency.

Jablin, F. M., Miller, V. D., & Keller, T. (1999). *Newcomer-leader role negotiations: Negotiation topics/issues, tactics, and outcomes.* Paper presented at the annual conference of the International Leadership Association, Atlanta, GA.

Jacobs, T. O. (1970). *Leadership and exchange in formal organizations.* Alexandria, VA: Human Resources Research Organization.

Johnston, W. B., & Packer, A. H. (1987). *Workforce 2000: Work and workers for the 21st century.* Indianapolis, IN: Hudson Institute.

Jones, J. (1985). *Labor of love, labor of sorrow: Black women, work, and the family from slavery to the present.* New York: Basic Books.

Kanter, R. M. (1977). *Men and women of the corporation.* New York: Basic Books.

Katz, D., & Kahn, R. L. (1966/1978). *The social psychology of organizations* (2nd ed.). New York: Wiley.

Kellerman, B. (1984). Leadership as a political act. In B. Kellerman (Ed.), *Leadership: Multidisciplinary perspectives* (pp. 63–89). Englewood Cliffs, NJ: Prentice Hall.

Kennedy, G. A. (1980). *Classical rhetoric.* Chapel Hill, NC: University of North Carolina Press.

Keto, C. T. (1989). *The Africa centered perspective of history.* Blackwood, NJ: KA Publications.

King, D. K. (1988). Multiple jeopardy, multiple consciousness: The context of a Black feminist ideology. *Signs, 14*(1), 42–72.

King, M. (1973). The politics of sexual stereotypes. *Black Scholar, 4,* 12–23.

Kochman, T. (1981). *Black and White styles in conflict.* Chicago: University of Chicago Press.

Kotter, J. P. (1982). *The general managers.* New York: Free Press.

Kouzes, J. M., & Posner, B. Z. (1995). *The leadership challenge.* San Francisco: Josey-Bass.

Ladson-Billings, G. (2000). Racialized discourses and ethnic epistemologies. In N. K. Denzin & Y. S. Lincoln (Eds.), *Handbook of Qualitative Research* (2nd ed., pp. 257–278). Thousand Oaks, CA: Sage.

Lerner, G. (1972). *Black women in White America: A documentary history.* New York: Vintage.

Loden, M. (1985). *Feminine leadership or: How to succeed in business without being one of the boys.* New Yori: Times Books.

Logan, S. W. (1999). *"We are coming": The persuasive discourse of nineteenth-century Black women.*

Lorde, A. (1984). *Sister outsider.* Trumansburg, NY: The Crossing Press.

Lubiano, W. (1992). Black ladies, welfare queens and state minstrels: Ideological war by narrative means. In T. Morrison (Ed.), *Race-ing justice, En-gendering power* (pp. 321–361). New York: Pantheon.

Lunneborg, P. (1990). *Women changing work.* Westport, CT: Greenwood Press.

Mainiero, L. (1994). Getting anointed for advancement: The case of executive women. The *Academy of Management Executive,* 8(2), 53–68.

Manz, C. C., & Sims, H. (1989). *Super-leadership.* New York: Prentice Hall.

Marshall, J. (1989). Re-envisioning career concepts: A feminist invitation. In M. B. Arthur, D. T. Hall, & B. S. Lawrence (Eds.), *Handbook of career theory* (pp. 275–291). Cambridge, UK: Cambridge University Press.

Marshall, J. (1993). Viewing organizational communication from a feminist perspective: A critique and some offerings. In S. Deetz (Ed.), *Communication Yearbook 16* (pp. 122–143). Newbury Park, CA: Sage.

Martin, J. (1992). *Cultures in organizations: Three perspectives.* New York: Oxford University Press.

Mathis, D. (2002). *Yet a stranger: Why Black Americans still don't feel at home.* New York: Warner Books.

May, S. K. (1997). Silencing the feminine in managerial discourse. Paper presented at the annual meeting of the National Communication Association, Chicago, IL.

McCluskey, A. T. (1997). "We specialize in the wholly impossible": Black women school founders and their mission. *Signs: Journal of women in Culture and Society, 22,* 403–426.

McGoldrick, M., Garcia-Preto, N., Hines, P. M., & Lee, E. (1988). Ethnicity and women. In M. McGoldrick, C. Anderson, & F. Walsh (Eds.), *Women in families* (pp. 169–199). New York: Norton.

Mead, G. H. (1934). *Mind, self, and society.* Chicago: University of Chicago Press.

Meindl, J. R., Ehrlich, S. B., & Dukerich, J. M. (1985). The romance of leadership. *Administrative Science Quarterly, 30,* 78–102.

Minnich, E. K. (1990). *Transforming knowledge.* Philadelphia: Temple University Press.

Mintzberg, H. (1973). *The nature of managerial work.* New York: Harper and Row.

Morgan, G. (1986). *Images of organization.* Beverly Hills, CA: Sage.

Morton, P. (1991). *Disfigured images: The historical assault on Afro-American women.* New York: Greenwood Press.

Mouffe, C. (1995). Feminism, citizenship, and radical democratic politics. In L. Nicholson & S. Seidman (Eds.), *Social postmodernism* (pp. 315–331). Cambridge, UK: Cambridge University Press.

Mumby, D. (1993). Feminism and the critique of organizational communication studies. In S. Deetz (Ed.), *Communication Yearbook 16* (pp. 155–166). Newbury Park, CA: Sage.

Mumby, D. K. (2001). Power and politics. In F. M. Jablin & L. L. Putnam (Eds.), *The new handbook of organizational communication: Advances in theory, research, and methods* (pp. 585–623). Newbury Park, CA: Sage.

Mumby, D. K., & Putnam, L. L. (1992). The politics of emotion: A feminist reading of bounded rationality. *Academy of Management Review, 17,* 465–486.

Nkomo, S. M. (1988). Race and sex: The forgotten case of the black female manager. In S. Rose & L. Larwood (Eds.), *Women's careers: Pathways and pitfalls* (pp. 133–150). New York: Praeger.

Nkomo, S. M. (1992). The emperor has no clothes: Rewriting "race in organizations." *Academy of Management Review, 17*(3), 487–513.

O'Brien Hallstein, D. L. (1997). A postmodern caring: Feminist standpoint theories, revisioned caring and communication ethics. *Western Journal of Communication, 63*(1), 32–56.

O'Brien Hallstein, D. L. (2000). Where standpoint stands now: An introduction and commentary. *Women's Studies in Communication, 23*(1), 1–15.

Omi, M., & Winant, H. (1986). *Racial formation in the United States: From the 1960s to the 1980s.*

Omolade, B. (1994). *The rising song of African American women.* New York: Routledge.

Orbe, M. P. (1998). Constructing co-cultural theory: An explication of culture, power, and communication. Thousand Oaks, CA: Sage.

Parker, P. S. (1997). *African American women executives within dominant culture organizations: An examination of leadership socialization, communication strategies, and leadership behavior.* Doctoral Dissertation, University of Texas at Austin (UMI No. 9802988).

Parker, P. S. (2001). African American Women Executives Within Dominant Culture Organizations: (Re)Conceptualizing notions of instrumentality and collaboration. *Management Communication Quarterly, 15*(1), 42–82.

Parker, P. S. (2002). Negotiating identity in Raced and Gendered Workplace Interactions: The use of strategic communication by African American Women senior executives within dominant culture organizations. *Communication Quarterly, 3*, 251–268.

Parker, P. S. (2003). Control, resistance, and empowerment in raced, gendered, and classed work contexts. *Communication Yearbook, 27* (pp. 257–301). Mahwah, NJ: Lawrence Erlbaum Associates.

Parker, P. S. & ogilvie, d. t. (1996). Gender, culture, and leadership: Toward a culturally distinct model of African-American women executives' leadership strategies. *Leadership Quarterly, 7*(2), 189–214.

Payne, C. M. (1995). *I've got the light of freedom: The organizing tradition and the Mississippi freedom Struggle.* Berkeley, CA: University of California Press.

Prasad, P. (1997). The Protestent ethic and the myths of the frontier: Cultural imprints, organizational structuring, and workplace diversity. In P. Prasad, A. J. Mills, M. Elmes, & A. Prasad (Eds.), *Managing the organizational melting pot: Dilemmas of workplace diversity* (pp. 129–147). Thousand Oaks, CA: Sage.

Prasad, P., Mills, A. J., Elmes, M., & Prasad, A. (Eds.). (1997). *Managing the organizational melting pot: Dilemmas of workplace diversity.* Thousand Oaks, CA: Sage.

Putnam, L. L., & Kolb, D. M. (2000). Rethinking exchange: Feminist views of communication and exchange. In P. Buzzanell (Ed.), *Rethinking organizational and managerial communication from feminist perspectives* (pp. 76–104). Thousand Oaks, CA: Sage.

Quint, C. I. (1970). *The role of American Negro women in the growth of the common school.* Unpublished doctoral dissertation, Brown University.

Radford-Hill, S. (2002). Keepin' it real: A generational commentary on Kimberly Springer's "Third wave Black feminism?" *Signs: A Journal of Women in Culture and Society, 27*(4), 1083–1090.

Rogers-Rose, L. (Ed.), (1980). *The Black woman* (pp. 217–232). Beverly Hills, CA: Sage.

Rosener, J. B. (1990). Ways women lead. *Harvard Business Review, 68*(6), 11–12.

Rost, J. C. (1991). *Leadership for the twenty-first century*. Westport, CT: Praeger.

Rowe, A. (2000). Locating feminism's subject: The paradox of White femininity and the struggle to forge feminist alliances. *Communication Theory, 10*(1), 64–80.

Schein, E. H. (1992), *Organizational culture and leadership* (2nd Ed.).San Francisco: Jossey-Bass.

Scott, J. (1986). Gender: A useful category of historical analysis. *American Historical Review, 91*, 1053–1075.

Seibold, D., & Shea, C. (2001). Participation and decision making. In F. M. Jablin & L. L. Putnam (Eds.), *The new handbook of organizational communication: Advances in theory, research, and methods* (pp. 664–703). Newbury Park, CA: Sage.

Senge, P. (1990). *The fifth discipline*. New York: Doubleday.

Senge, P., Kleiner, A., Roberts, C., Ross, R., Roth, G., & Smith, B. (1999). *The dance of change: The challenge to sustaining momentum in learning organizations*. New York: Doubleday.

Shuter, R., & Turner, L. H. (1997). African American and European American women in the workplace: Perceptions of workplace communication. *Management Communication Quarterly, 11*(1), 74–96.

Sims, H. P., Jr., & Manz, C. C. (1996). *Company of heroes: Unleashing the power of self-leadership*. New York: John Wiley.

Smircich, L., & Morgan, G. (1982). Leadership and the management of meaning. *Journal of Applied Behavioral Science, 18*, 257–273.

Smircich, L., & Stubbart, C. (1985). Strategic management in an enacted world. *Academy of Management Review, 10*, 724–736.

Smith, D. (1987). *The everyday world as problematic*. Boston: Northeastern University Press.

Spelman, E. (1988). *Inessential woman: Problems of exclusion in feminist thought*. Boston: Beacon Press.

Springer, K. (1999). *Still lifting, still climbing: African American women's contemporary activism*. New York: New York University Press.

Stinchcombe, A. L. (1965). Social structure and organizations. In J. G. March (Ed.), *Handbook of organizations* (pp, 142–193). Chicago, Rand McNally.

Stack, C. B. (2000). Different voices, different visions: Gender, culture, and moral reasoning. In M.. B. Zinn, P. Hondagneu-Sotelo, & M. Messner (Eds.), *Gender through the prism of difference* (2nd ed., pp. 42–48). Boston: Allyn and Bacon.

Stall, S., & Stoecker, R. (1998). Community organizing or organizing community? Gender and the crafts of empowerment. *Gender & Society, 12*(6), 729–756.

Stohl, C., & Cheney, G. (2001). Participatory processes/paradoxical practices. Communication and the dilemmas of organizational democracy. *Management Communication Quarterly 14*, 349–407.

Strauss, A., & Corbin, J. (1990). *Basics of qualitative research: Grounded theory procedures and techniques*. Newbury Park, CA: Sage.

Tannen, D. (1990). *You just don't understand: Women and men in conversation*. New York: William Morrow.

Taylor, B. C., & Trujillo, N. (2001). Qualitative research methods. In F. M. Jablin & L. L. Putnam (Eds.), *The new handbook of organizational communication: Advances in theory, research, and methods* (pp. 161–194). Thousand Oaks, CA: Sage.

Thomas, D., & Gabarro, J. J. (1999). *Breaking through: The making of minority executives in corporate America*. Boston: Harvard Business School Press.

Tichy, N., & DeVanna, M. (1986). *The transformational leader*. New York: Wiley.

Ting-Toomey, S. (1986). Conflict communication styles in Black and White Subjective Cultures. In W. Gudykunst & Y. Kim (Eds.), Interethnic communication (pp. 7–88). Newbury Park, CA: Sage.

Trethewey, A. (1997). Resistance, identity, and empowerment: A postmodern feminist analysis of clients in a human service organization. Communication Monographs, 64, 281–301.

Trethewey, A. (2000). Revisioning control: A feminist critique of disciplined bodies. In P. Buzzanell (Ed.), Rethinking organizational and managerial communication from feminist perspectives (pp. 107–127). Thousand Oaks, CA: Sage.

Twine, F. W. (2000). Feminist fairy tales for Black and American Indian girls: A working-class vision. Signs: Journal of Women in Culture and Society, 25(4), 1227–1230.

Walker, A. (1983). In search of our mothers' gardens. New York: Harcourt Brace Jovanovich.

Vaz, K. M. (Ed.). (1995). Black Women in America (pp. 159–178). Thousand Oaks, CA: Sage.

Warren, K. B., & Bourque, S. C. (1991). Women, technology, and development ideologies: analyzing feminist voices, In M. di Leonardo (Ed.), Gender at the crossroads of knowledge: Feminist anthropology in the postmodern era (pp. 278–311). Berkeley, CA: University of California.

Weick, K. (1978). The spines of leaders. In M. W. McCall & M. Lombardo (Eds.), Leadership, where else can we go? (pp. 37–61). Durham, NC: Duke University Press.

Weitz, R., & Gordon, L. (1993). Images of Black women among Anglo college students. Sex Roles, 28, 19–34.

Welter, B. (1966). The cult of true womanhood, 1820–60. American Quarterly, 18, 151–74.

Welton, K. (1997). Nancy Hartsock's standpoint theory: From content to "concrete multiplicity." Women & Politics, 18(3), 7–24.

Wheatley, M. (1992). Leadership and the new science. San Francisco: Berrett-Koehler.

White, D. G. (1985). Ar'n't I a woman? Female slaves in the plantation South. New York: W. W. Norton.

Williams, J., & Dixie, Q. (2003). This far by faith: Stories from the African American religious experience. New York: William Morrow.

Williams, L. E. (2002). Servants of the people: The 1960s legacy of African American leadership. New York: St. Martin's Press.

Witherspoon, P. D. (1997). Communicating leadership: An organizational perspective. Boston: Allyn & Bacon.

Wood, J. T. (1994). Who cares: Women, care, and culture. Carbondale, IL: Southern Illinois University Press.

Wood, J. T. (1998). Gendered lives: Communication, gender and culture (2nd ed.). Belmont: Wadsworth.

Yoder, J. D., & Aniakudo, P. (1997, June). "Outsider within" the firehouse: Subordination and difference in the social interactions of African American women firefighters. Gender & Society, 11(3), 324–41.

Yukl, G. (2002). Leadership in organizations (5th ed.). Upper Saddle River, NJ: Prentice Hall.

Author Index

Subject Index

Note: n indicates endnote, *t* indicates table

A

Abolitionist movement, 41, 51
African American, xxiiin3
    community, 86–87
      leaders, 50
    co-workers, 62, 90
    children, 41, 49–50
    employees, 86
    girls, 92
    life, 37
    preachers, 50
    urban neighborhoods, 46
African American/Black men 11, 41, 45, 48
    as religious leaders, 42
    resistance strategies of, 37, 40–41
    traditional roles of, 36
    working, 49
African American/Black women, xxiiin3
    as marginal workers, xxii, 44-48
    as natural laborers, xxii, 36
    contributions of, 30–31
    derogatory images of, 34–36
    devaluation of, 30, 31, 34-36, 45, 47-48, 71
    discrimination targeting, 22
    domestic servants, xxivn4
    enslaved, 34–37, 39-41
    entrepreneurs, 45
    executives, xii, xiii, 24, 59, 66, 72, 73, 78, 85, 87, 90, 93, 95, 97
    factory workers, 47–48
    gender identity of, 10
    heads of households, 46–47
    history of, 29–32, 67-68, 87, 91-92
    in professions, 53
    leadership roles of, 41, 51–52
    media portrayal of, 30
    negative stereotypes of, 16, 30, 34–36, 97
    19th century, 39
    oppression of, 24, 40
    work experiences of, 31
African American/Black women's
    achievements, 38
    clubs, 49–52
    communication style, 68–70, 72, 78
    embodied identities, 10
    gifts, 30
    history in America, 29–32
    labor force participation, 34, 47–48
    leadership experiences, xiv–xv, xx, xxii, 4, 10, 27, 31–34, 43–44, 48–49 57, 68–69, 72, 73, 93
    participation in women's rights movements, 39, 50–51, 53
    resistance to oppressive discourses, 31–32, 92
    strategies for empowerment, 37
    standpoints, 16
    strategies for
      change during era of slavery, 36-40
      survival, 38, 48–49